A HISTORY OF MAIDENHEAD

ST. MARY'S CHAPEL AND CHAPEL ARCHES, 1820.

A HISTORY OF
MAIDENHEAD

J. WESLEY WALKER

THAMES VALLEY PRESS
MAIDENHEAD 1971

Reproduced and Printed in Great Britain by
Redwood Press Limited
Trowbridge & London

INTRODUCTORY CHAPTER
TO 1971 EDITION

I am one of the fortunate few who are in possession of one of the earlier editions of Mr. Walker's book. Not a first edition admittedly but a later and enlarged version printed in the year 1931. The copy that I own belonged at one time to a local dignatory and contains an inscription written by the author which reads—'Maidenhead is my native town. It has been my good fortune to be associated with its public and commercial life. To write its history has been a labour of love'. This, indeed, must have been the case, as embarking on such a work would seem arduous to one who was not devoted to his subject, as was J. Wesley Walker. As one reads the book, one can detect the affection that the author had for Maidenhead, and suspects that he would dearly have loved to have been present at some of the more colourful events in the Town's history.

Although the second largest town in Berkshire, Maidenhead has never been particularly rich in history. Unlike Reading, Wallingford, Abingdon, Wantage or Windsor; the town cannot boast of a very early foundation, or of any events which have seriously influenced the history of the nation. Nevertheless, like every community, it has its story to tell, and Mr. Walker has presented this story, successfully and concisely in the pages that follow. As an historical work, it contributes towards an account of the nation as a whole, and as such is an invaluable record.

In the age of motorways and shopping precincts, records of the past are essential. Local societies work frantically to preserve what they can in the face of inevitable progress. The ever growing population demands more housing and supermarkets and the phenomenal increase in motorised transport necessitates the building of better roads and the provision of additional car parking facilities. Land is at a premium, and office blocks must go upwards and not outwards, thus requiring deeper foundations on which to build. Maidenhead has very few scheduled buildings, therefore, many unprotected edifices bearing links with the town's past, have fallen victim to the mechanical bulldozer.

Over the past twenty years the face of Maidenhead has changed considerably. Most of the prominent buildings which existed at the time this book was written have now disappeared. The Guildhall, erected in 1770 at a cost of £1330, and once dominating the town centre, was replaced in 1962 by the new Town Hall at a cost of £400,000. This was brought about by the Corporation in an attempt to centralise all local government departments. The Borough Church of St. Andrew and Mary Magdalene, on which Mr. Walker lavishes two chapters, was pulled down in 1963 and rebuilt in brick and glass on the same site. This represents the third rebuilding of the chapel since its foundation in 1270, the situation at one time being much nearer to the Chapel Arches, which explains the

vii

derivation of the name. The new modern church was consecrated in April 1965 by the Lord Bishop of Oxford and is a handsome building, even if it does lack the character of the original.

At the time of writing a new Public Library is being constructed adjacent to the old building, which necessitated the removal of the War Memorial to a new site outside the Town Hall, under a storm of disapproval. The original Library was opened in 1904, and during its existence has housed the exhibits known as 'Maidenhead Museum' the sad remnants of which can be found in the basement of the Town Hall. Traffic congestion in the town has now reached a peak, and the construction of a new relief road has caused a major upheaval of the old road system and the destruction of many more buildings including the Wesley Hall, the Pearce Hall and St. Pauls Church. Alas, the Maidenhead that J. Wesley Walker knew is crumbling around us, and if he were able to see the town, as it is to-day, he would surely be very sad indeed.

Mr. Walker's evidence of the early history of Maidenhead is perhaps a little scanty, and his interpretation based on reports of early anti-quaries is now somewhat outdated. The advance of archaeological research over the past forty years has enabled us to see the position more clearly and re-examine earlier evidence. It is true to say that Maidenhead did not exist as a town before the Medieval Period and indeed, did not receive its first Charter of Incorporation until 1582. The area, however, has always been attractive to early man, and the hunter-fisher-men of the early Stone Age built their homes on the gravel terraces of the Thames and then later by the river itself. Important evidence of the first of these cultures has been found at Furze Platt, Boyn Hill and elsewhere, and is repre-sented by Stone Axes manufactured from local flint. Existence of the later Mesolithic cultures has been found at Braywick and Bray, where a whole range of microliths and associated imple-ments have been located. Finds of the Bronze and Iron Ages are fairly evenly spread across the area from Cookham to Bray, and metal objects of these periods have been dredged from the river. Just prior to the Roman invasion, the Belgae built the earthwork known as Robin Hood's Arbour on Maidenhead Thicket. During the Roman period the area surrounding Maiden-head was given over to farming, controlled from a series of Villas situated at intervals of perhaps one and a half miles. Apart from the Castle Hill Villa mentioned by Mr. Walker, several others are known to exist including one which was excavated in 1960 at Cox Green. Small Roman settlements probably existed at Bray and Waltham St. Lawrence but not on the current site of Maidenhead Town. The Roman road crossing Kidwells Park, which is mentioned by Mr. Walker has been examined recently and there is much to suggest that it may be a bank of natural gravel. Evidence of the Saxon period is adequately covered in this book, but mention should be made of the early Medieval long-house excavated recently on a moated site at Spencers Farm, North Town. The house is connected with the Manor of Spencers or Knight Ellington, and probably belonged to the bailiff who administered the estate for his Lord. Mr. Walker mentions the Manor in the first chapter of the book.

The later history of the town taken from documentary evidence dating back to the Medieval period, is very fully recorded in this book, and the author must be admired for his patience in assembling so much interesting and amusing material from so many sources. I understand that there are plans afoot to publish a new history of Maidenhead, which will cover events up to the present day, but until such time as it becomes available, this book will remain the only definitive work on the subject.

LUKE OVER
May 1971

PREFATORY NOTE TO THE SECOND EDITION

THE favourable reception accorded to the first edition of this work resulted in the offer to the writer of a considerable amount of additional information from private sources. This, together with other material from public, or semi-public sources which has since come to hand, will be found incorporated in the following pages.

Amongst those to whom the writer is indebted, and to whom his grateful acknowledgments are presented, he would especially desire to mention the late Sir George Young, Bart., the Rev. C. E. M. Fry (Rural Dean), Professor Stenton, of Reading University, and Mr. H. E. Bannard, of Littlewick.

J. W. W.

April, 1931.

PREFACE

IF Maidenhead has not been specially rich in history, it has been still less rich in historians. With the exception of the Rev. G. C. Gorham's scholarly account of St. Mary's Chapel and Chantry, but little has been written beyond a few notices in Gazetteers and Itineraries, and even these notices have not always been remarkable for their accuracy. Possibly if the town had been privileged to play a more striking part in English History, its life and growth would have been more fully recorded. Yet every town, like every individual life, has its story. It has felt the influence of each successive age, and in turn has more or less directly re-acted upon it; and as trivial incidents will frequently throw light on greater events, so the details of the life of a small town may enable us the better to understand the history of a nation.

The present volume is an attempt to gather up such fragments of Maidenhead's history as are not yet lost, and to preserve the past for the use of the future. The readiness to afford information and render assistance which the writer has met with on all hands in the discharge of his task, leads him to believe that there are many who think with him as to the desirability of preserving the memorials of by-gone days, even though the events to be recorded are more often of local than national significance.

It is, perhaps, too much to hope that certain inaccuracies which have been repeated for two hundred years will now be repeated no more, but it is really time they were laid to rest. It is *not* true that Edward III. granted the first charter of incorporation; Queen Margaret did *not* found St. Mary's; and, with Mr. Darby, I greatly fear the Vicar of Hurley did *not* receive extra pay for braving the dangers of Maidenhead Thicket, though we have had these statements dinned into us continually. Each of these points will be found fully dealt with in its appropriate place, and the Authorities given for the conclusion arrived at. And, indeed, if this volume has any permanent value, it will probably be found in the fact that no statement of importance is made without giving the authority or reference.

To the Mayor and Corporation of Maidenhead for permission to search and utilise the Corporation muniments; to the Clergy and Ministers who have given access to their churches and records; to the Secretaries of various Societies; to all who have assisted by the loan of books or documents; to those who have favoured with personal reminiscences of the past, and of these especially to Alderman Richard Silver, whose memory of by-gone Maidenhead is as fresh as his years—92—are venerable, the writer desires to present his grateful acknowledgments.

J. W. W.

December, 1909.

CONTENTS

APPENDIX

ILLUSTRATIONS

AUTHORITIES AND REFERENCES

B.B.O.	Berks, Bucks, and Oxon Archæological Journal.
B.C.R.	Bray Court Rolls.
Bridge M & C	Minutes, Cash Accounts, and Register of Mortgages of Mayor, Bridge-masters, &c., relating to Maidenhead Bridge, from 1772 to 1835 (Corporation Muniments) 7 Vols.
Br. Mus. or B.M.	British Museum.
Cal. St. Pap. Dom.	Calendar of the State Papers. Domestic Series.
Cal. Tres. B & P	Calendar of the Treasury Books and Papers.
V.C.H.	Victoria County History of Berkshire.
C.C.R.	Cookham Court Rolls.
Dic. Nat. Biog.	Dictionary of National Biography.
Extracts	Extracts from the Records of the Corporation, Minutes, &c., relating to the taking down and rebuilding of the Chapel of St. Andrew and St. Mary Magdalene. (Compiled by Isaac Pocock) 1826. Preserved in Maidenhead Public Library, 942.29.
Gorham	An Account of the Chapel, Chauntry, and Guild of Maidenhead by the Rev. G. C. Gorham, B.D.
Kerry	History and Antiquities of the Hundred of Bray by Charles Kerry, 1861.

Leland	Leland's Itinerary.
Maid.	The Muniments of the Maidenhead Corporation preserved at the Town Hall and calendared under various letters. Thus, " Maid J 115 " signifies Document No. 115 in bundle J in the Corporation Deed Chest.
M·F.C.	Reports of the Maidenhead Field Club preserved in the Maidenhead Public Library.
Municip. Corp. Rep.	Municipal Corporations Commissioners' Report. 1835 Vol. IV. pp. 2909-16.
Powys	Passages from the Diaries of Mrs. Philip Lybbe Powys.
Rot. Claus.	Calendar of the Close Rolls.
Rot. Pat.	Calendar of the Patent Rolls.
Cox	Personal reminiscences contributed by Alderman C. W. Cox, J.P.
Mackie	Do. by Alderman Mackie, J.P.
Silver	Do. by Alderman Richard Silver, J.P.
Walker	Do. by Robert Walker, Esqre., J.P.
Young	Do. by Sir George Young, Bart.

INDEX

CHAPTER I.

EARLY HISTORY AND NAME.

AIDENHEAD is situated 26 miles from London on the great Bath Road, in the County of Berks, on the banks of the Thames, where that river separates Berkshire from Buckinghamshire. Though now a parish of itself, having been so constituted on October 15th, 1894, its northern half is in the ancient parish of Cookham, its southern portion in the ancient parish and hundred of Bray, the line of demarcation being the road from London to the West, which from Maidenhead Bridge bears for some three miles the consecutive names of Bridge Road, Bridge Street, High Street, and Castle (formerly Folly) Hill.

Local prehistoric remains are not numerous, yet they are not without interest, for it was in a pit close by the Dumb Bell at Taplow, in the lower drift level, that the Rev. C. Kingsley and Mr. John Lubbock (Lord Avebury) made in 1855 the important discovery of a skull of a Musk Ox (*Ovibos moschatus*), now in the British Museum, and thus afforded the first proof of the existence of this animal in Britain. The remains of the mammoth (*elephas primogenius*), the horse (*equus caballus* and *fossilis*), and the rhinoceros (*tichorhinus*) have also been found in the same locality.

Although Maidenhead makes no appearance

V. C. H. I. 25.

M. F. C. Rep. 8 p. 40.

as a town prior to the Norman Conquest, Celtic, Roman, Saxon, and other remains testify to a district more or less populous long prior to that event. Probably the higher levels around Maidenhead were those first favoured by our ancestors, local antiquarians having located " hut circles "

M. F. C.
Rep. VIII. 17.

or " pit dwellings " both at Taplow and Maidenhead Thicket. By the time of the Roman occupation the population had drawn nearer the

Leland.

river. The district was inhabited by the Bibroci, who were subdued by the Romans, and were amongst the first of the Celtic tribes to submit to their conquerors. But British earthworks on Maidenhead Thicket, where an embankment has been traced 5 feet high, 10 feet in diameter, and 80 yards long, doubtless the remains of a British fort, testify that the submission was not without a struggle.

The Romans have left several memorials of their occupation. A Roman road crosses High Street and West Street at right angles, proceeding due north and south, and may be distinctly traced across Kidwell's Park and on towards Cookham; but the most important relic of this

M. F. C.
Report 8 p. 50.

time unquestionably is the Roman Villa, discovered in 1886 on land on Castle Hill belonging to Mr. R. Silver, which was carefully explored at the time by Mr. James Rutland, F.G.S. Mr. Rutland was of opinion that the building had originally been of considerable proportions. Among the remains were coins of Tetricus (A.D. 267-273), pieces of Samian Ware, portions of over sixty vessels of Roman and British pottery, and, in what was probably the kitchen midden, bones

of sheep, pigs, deer, and other animals. Some
of the tiles and bricks bore foot marks as if some
animal, and in one case a man, had walked over
them before they had been hardened. The various
rooms of the house could be traced with more or
less certainty, the bathing and heating arrangements being very evident. Such of the remains
as could be conveniently removed, including the
leaden pipe from the bath, were presented by
Mr. Silver to the Town Museum.

During the Saxon wars Berkshire was for 300 V. C. H. II. 116.
years a " buffer state " between Mercia and the
West Saxons. Doubtless its sons then, as in all
subsequent wars, sent their contingent to the
battle, but such times were not favourable for
building up communities. It is not therefore
till the days of the Domesday Book that Maidenhead appears as a separate place with its own
name of South Ellington, a name which it bore Kerry 135.
till 1296, when that designation disappears from
the records of the Bray Court Rolls and gives
place to the present title.

The Domesday statement is as follows :— V. C. H. I. 356.

" In Benes (Beynhurst) Hundred. The same
Ghilo holds Elenstone. Siward held it T. R. E.
[temp. reg. Ed.] Then as now [it was assessed]
at 3 hides. There is land for 4 ploughs. Two
men hold of Ghilo : Hugh and Landri. They
have there 2 ploughs : and [there are] 6 villeins
and 4 cottars with 1 plough. There are 16 acres
of meadow and woodland to render 10 swine. It
was [formerly] worth 60 shillings; now 40
shillings."

To this the Victoria County History of Berks appends the following Note :—

'In *Testa de Nevill* (p. 121), all these holdings of Ghilo appear (except Enborne) as the fief of Henry de Pinkney. In *Feudal Aids* 1428 i 70 we have 1 Knight's fee and also ½ a Knight's fee in "Northelyntone " held by John Pynkenye. Camden in *Britannia* (Eng. translation of 1610 p. 286) speaks of a little town named in the former ages " Southealington afterward Maidenhith and at this day Mai(n)denhead " (the ' n ' seems to be a misprint). These taken together give the position of Elentone as Maidenhead and Pinkney's Green.'

How or why Maidenhead got its present name no mortal knows. Suggestions are plentiful, but certainty is yet to seek. Edmunds connects it with Maid, the Virgin Mary; Leland, who visited Maidenhead in 1538, derives it from a head of one of the 11,000 virgins who followed St. Ursula and were slaughtered at Cologne; Ditchfield thinks Maiden means Mai-den (or Mai Dun) the fortified hill; Isaac Taylor, rejecting such interpretations as the " wharf by the meadow," and the " timber wharf," from " mœd " Anglo Saxon a tree trunk, explained it as Mayden hithe, the middle wharf between Marlow [? Hedsor] and Windsor; while another suggestion is Maiden-hithe or the new wharf. On the whole it seems fairly established that the first part of the word is from the Old English form of " Maiden," but what particular meaning should be given to it is uncertain, as the word is used in several place names with differing

Edmunds'
Traces of
History in
Histories, 183,
the Names of
Places, 248.

Names and
their
Words and
Places, 411.

significations. The second element may be rendered either by the Old English " hatch " or " hythe," but the balance of the argument appears to favour " hythe," a landing place. Leland's fancy may be dismissed at once.

When Maidenhead first used its present name is also a matter of doubt. It was in use in 1273, Rot. Pat. as in November of that year Reginald de Maidenhuth, Canon of Holy Cross, Waltham, brought news to Edward I. of the death of the Abbot Richard, and in the following January was himself elected to the vacant office. It may be remarked that the correct spelling of the town's name seemed for many years as doubtful as its origin. A list of some of the many orthographical variations is given in Appendix A.

Although we cannot accept Leland's suggestion as to the derivation of the name of the town, his quaint account of his visit to Maidenhead in 1538 must not be omitted.

" A ii. or iii. miles beyond the passage over Leland. Burne, I cam to Maidenhed bridge of tymbre upon the Tamise.

" A little above the bridge, ripa citeriori Tamesis, I saw a cliffy ground as hanging over the Tamise, and sum busschis groinge on it. I conjectid that ther had beene sum site of an ancient building.

" There is a grete warfeage of tymbre and fierwood on the west ende of the bridge; and this wood cummith out of Barkshir and the great woddis of the forest of Windelsore and the greate frithe.

(Heere mark that as much ground as

lyith bytwixt the arme of colne that goith thoroug Colebroke toun and the bridge of Maidenhed is yn Bukkinghamshur. Beyond is Barkeshir.)

" The toun of Maidenhed stondith a praty distance from the Tamise side, and is meately welle buildid. The south side of the toune is in the Paroche of Bray.

" The north side is yn the Paroch of Cokeham.

" From Maidenhedde town a ii. miles by a narrow wooddy way to the Frithe. And so thorough the Frithe iii. miles and more. And then to Twyford, a praty tounlet, a ii. miles."

MAIDENHEAD BRIDGE.

The "Orkney Arms" (later "Skindlés") is shown on the right.

CHAPTER II.

THE BRIDGE.

MAIDENHEAD dates its rise and the commencement of its prosperity from the building of its first bridge over the Thames, somewhere about 1280. Prior to that a ford, or ferry, doubtless existed at the same spot, as is evidenced by the many interesting " finds " of ancient implements and weapons discovered there. But the main road to the West did not go through Maidenhead. It branched off to the North at Two Mile Brook V. C. H.
I. 376. through Burnham, then a market town, over Taplow Common, through Cliveden Woods, crossed the river at Babham End, went through Cookham (a market town valued at £1 per annum at the time of the Domesday Survey), and on to Maidenhead Thicket, where it diverged, one part going to Reading and Bristol and the West, and one to Henley and Gloucester.

The new bridge diverted the traffic from Burnham and Cookham, and a new wharf gave increased facilities for trade, and so it came to pass that the little hamlet of South Ellington developed into the town of Maidenhead.

The bridge was probably much longer than its successor, and its centre arch was the point of meeting of the parishes of Cookham, Bray Rutland
M. F. C.
1891. and Taplow, as was testified by depositions taken in Maidenhead before Sir Henry Nevyll,

John Goodwyn, and Roland Hynde, 16th June, 1578; William Norres, defendant, against Henry Manfield, of Amerden, complainant. It was a wooden structure, and was continually getting out of repair during the whole course of its history, to say nothing of its sufferings in times of war when again and again it was broken down. Reference to this occurs several times in the State Papers. Thus, on 25th September, 1644, the Earl of Manchester writes to the Committee of both Kingdoms that he " was constrained to wait at Uxbridge as Maidenhead Bridge was broken," and adds he will march as soon as with any conveniency he can.

Two days later the Earl writes : " This day most of my forces are to pass over at Maidenhead, which they could not have done sooner."

Again, on 30th November, 1688, Thomas Oldfield, a Bristol solicitor, writes to Sir John Newton that he is informed " the bridges at Staines, Kingston, Windsor and Maidenhead are to be broken down."

For its repair, and maintenance grants of pontage, or tolls, were repeatedly made by the sovereign, the earliest on record bearing date 4th December, 1297, where Edward I. makes a " grant at the instance of William de Berford in aid of the Bridge of Maydenheth, which is almost broken down, of pontage for three years, to be taken by the hands of two good and lawful men appointed by him." Many similar grants were made by subsequent monarchs. One by Edward III., dated 22nd October, 1337, gives the tariff. It is a " grant to the bailiffs and good men of

Marginal notes:

Leland.

Cal. St.
Pap. Dom.

Br. Mus.
Bar. T.
5 a.

Rot. Pat.

Rot. Pat.

Maidenhithe of pontage 1d. every cartload of merchandise over bridge and 1d. every ship or boat laden with merchandise under it, to be taken for 6 years by William de Walden and William le Housebond.''

In addition to pontage, the bridge benefited from a very singular custom that prevailed largely in the middle ages. Hermitages were established on or adjoining various bridges, where certain men duly licenced by the bishop of the diocese dwelt as hermits, receiving gifts from passers-by, and, after taking for themselves only so much as sufficed for their bare sustenance, handing over the surplus for the upkeep of the bridge. These hermits were sworn to a life of renunciation and devotion. Sometimes they were priests, sometimes laymen. Occasionally an elaborately fitted chapel formed part of the bridge erection, otherwise the hermitage was of a humbler description. Such an arrangement prevailed at Maidenhead. The hermitage chapel is described as adjoining the bridge (*juxta pontem*) on the west side, and as having been "rebuilt" in 1423. It was probably in connexion with this re-building that a contribution was made from Abingdon, entered in the old notebook of John Huchyns, "Also I payd to the Brygge of Maydynhythe xxd." Huchyns was an active member of the Fraternity of the Holy Cross, though it is not quite certain whether the donation came from the funds of the Fraternity, or from an estate of which he was the executor. The Salisbury Registers give in some fulness an account of the induction of a hermit at Maiden-

Sarum Epis. Reg. Chandler fol: 40, 41.

Cal C. H. Hosp. Abingdon.

head. It was on 29th October, 1423, when John, Warden of the Collegiate Church of Shottesbrook, duly armed with the Commission of the Bishop of Salisbury, came over to Maidenhead to admit Richard Ludlow to the hermitage at the bridge, if after enquiry he should be found a man of honest conversation and laudable life. The Warden of Shottesbrook, doubtless accompanied by divers of his officials, and probably with some insignia of office, was met by Andrew Sperling, who though Mayors and Municipal Wardens had not yet been known in Maidenhead, yet being Steward of the Manors of Bray and Cookham held a position of authority, and seems to have been the great man of the town. With him came John Mustard, the beadle, in all his glory, and John Coter and Robert, the chaplains, Thomas and John Palmer, the bailiffs (procuratores), and quite a company of the prominent men of the town and neighbourhood, amongst whom were James Lynde, John Pynkeney, Thomas Lettford, John Louches, — Skynner, Simon Norton, John Lawrence, and Richard Bullock, and many others. It is easy to imagine the procession wending its way down the old street, and taking up its position at the entrance of the "rebuilt" hermitage by the bridge. Then Richard Ludlow stands forth, and amidst the solemn silence of the spectators recites the following oath :—

"In the name of God Amen. I, Richard Ludlow, byfore God and you commissary of my reverend lord and fader Johan by grace of God, Bisshop of Salisbury, and also in presence of all these worshipful

men here beyng, I oppon by profession of
heremite under this forme that I the foresaid Richard make protestation and by
note fro this day forward to be obedient
to god and to holye churche havynge
ye mynstres profession in worship and
reverence; Also to lede my lyf to my
lyves ende in well continente and chastitie,
and to eschew all open spectacles, commone
scotales and tavernys which yt bey unlawful and forbodyn by holy church and all
other suspect placis of Synne, furthermore
I graunte on my profession every day to
here masse and to sey every day continually onyce our lady Sauter, and on
Sundays and other holidays to say our
lady Sauter, and also XV pater nosters
and aves in ye worship and mynd of the
woundys that oure lord suffered for me
and all mankynde, Also to faste every
Firday in ye yere and ye vigils of pentecost
and alle Halweyn and ye fyve vigils of oure
lady to bred and water, and this foresaid
observance as of heryng masse, praying
and fastyng, I shal kepe treuly, but ef het
be so that any gret sykness or travaile or
any other resonable lette or impediment
the which may not be eschewed by cause
of my lettyng, and yt ye godes yt I may
gete othir by some gift of cristen people
or by quest or testament othir by eny othir
resonable and trew wey recevyng only
necessarie to my Sustinaunce as in mete,
drink, cloth, and fuell, I shall trewly wt

owte deceyte uppon reparacion and amend-
yng of the brigg and of ye common weyes
longing to ye same town of Maydenhith."

This is followed by a brief Latin office
blessing the hermit's habit, and indicating how
it symbolised the wearer's humility of heart and
contempt of the world. This done, the formal
word is spoken, Richard Ludlow is the Hermit
of Maidenhead, and Warden and Hermit and
Chaplains and townsmen crowd, as many of them
as can, into the little chapel, where an act of
devotion concludes the strange ceremony. Henceforth Richard Ludlow will take such alms as
passers over Maidenhead bridge will give him,
or as others may bequeath to him, will keep only
what is " necessarie to his sustinaunce," and all
the rest will be spent on the bridge and the roads.

Maid
Char. 3.

In addition to pontage and the gifts to the
hermit, the town acquired the right by the
Charter of James I. to take three oak trees yearly
from the Royal Manors of Cookham and Bray
for bridge repairs, and the State Papers show
that the men of Maidenhead were not negligent
in reminding the authorities of this right. Under
date of 11th May, 1654, Col. Whitcote and

Cal. St. Pap.
Dom.

Thomas Reading report to Cromwell that
"the Warden and Bridgemasters of Maidenhead
demand 3 trees, and 4 which they said became
due during the war, when they durst not repair
their bridges which were several times broken
down to prevent the enemy passing." A certified
extract from the Charter of James I. accompanied

Cal. St. Pap.
Dom.

this report. There is also calendared 21st
January, 1676, a "claim by the Town of Maiden-

head of their right to take oaks " for bridge reparation. In the ".Treasury Books and Papers" Cal. Treas. B. & P. there is a petition dated 5th May, 1714, from the Corporation to the Lord Treasurer, stating that the oaks to which they were entitled were of small value, and their tolls were much lessened by a free bridge erected by the Queen (Anne) at Datchett, and praying for a grant of " such of the dotard and pollard trees as the exigencies of their town required." Another petition on 8th June, 1732, did not forget to mention the Cal. Treas. B. & P. loss by reason of Datchett free bridge. As it was followed the next year, 13th April, 1735, by a Treasury Order for *twenty* oaks for the repair of the bridge, it may be taken that the petitioners did not appeal in vain.

The old bridge was repaired on a substantial scale for the last time in 1750, when on 12th March an agreement was entered into by Mr. Stiff Leadbetter to execute the necessary works for £600. The agreement is a formidable document, and is still preserved amongst the Corporation muniments, as is also the final receipted bill, Maid: I. 74. which shows that the amount paid in the end was £764 9s. 2d. Twenty years later it was felt that something more than repairing must be done. The condition of the structure was Maid: R. 194. seriously considered in a series of meetings from 5th October, 1770, to 18th January, 1771, when it was resolved to apply to Parliament for power to build an entirely new bridge. Plans were submitted by Mr. Fuller White for a wooden structure, and by Mr. (afterwards Sir) Robert Taylor for a stone one. The act of Parliament for building the new bridge was passed, and read to the Corporation on 23rd May, 1772, when also Mr. Taylor's plans were formally accepted.

The architect was a man of some eminence in his profession. Lincoln's Inn was one of his works, and he was also employed to carry out certain additions to the Bank of England. He it was, too, who sculptured the monuments to Cornwall and Guest in Westminster Abbey. Knighthood was conferred on him in 1782 during his year of office as Sheriff of London, and his name is perpetuated in Oxford by the Taylorian Institute, of which he was the founder. He was born in 1714 and died in 1788.

The contractor was Mr. John Townsend of Oxford, with whom an engagement was signed on 3rd July, 1772. The contract price was £14,500, and Mr. Townsend entered into a bond of £5,000 for due preformance. The whole of the documents, including plans, detail drawings, contract, and bond, are preserved with the Borough muniments.

By the time it was finished Mr. Townsend's account had risen to £15,741 1s. 10½d., and this sum was paid to him. Sir Robert Taylor, for his services as architect and Surveyor, received £1,200. When to these items are added the Clerk's expenses, which amounted to several hundreds of pounds, and various sums for incidental works on special fencing, removal of certain houses, &c., the total cost cannot have been much under £19,000, besides what was paid for additional land for the approaches. The whole of the structure and approaches are by the

Bridge Act of 1772 in the County of Berks, and in the Parish of Bray, and occupy a position slightly to the South of the older bridge, the remains of which were still to be seen for more than one hundred years later. The work was five years in completing, a period which the Corporation thought much too long, and the minutes indicate a considerable amount of irritation at the Contractor's delay. The foundation Stone was laid by the Mayor on the 19th October, 1772, and a copper plate let into the stone bore the following inscription :—

THIS FOUNDATION STONE

OF

MAIDENHEAD BRIDGE

was laid on the 19th day of October in the year of our Lord, 1772,

in the twelfth year of the reign of His Majesty, King George the Third,

by James Atlee, Esq., Mayor,

in the presence of the Corporation of Maidenhead.

Penyston Powney, Esq., High Steward.

Robert Vansittart, Esq., Recorder.

John Gould ⎫
John Boult ⎬ Bridgemasters.

Henry Emblin ⎫
James Adams ⎪
Richard Withall ⎪
John Hall ⎪
William Rose ⎬ Burgesses.
Henry Lovegrove ⎪
John Clark ⎪
Richard Taylor ⎭

James Payne, Town Clerk.

Architect, Robert Taylor, Esq.

Mason, John Townsend.

The centre arch was turned on 5th May, 1775, when a guinea was distributed amongst the workmen, and the bridge was opened on 22nd August,

Maid: I. 64, p. 270.

1777, when a " feast " was held in honour of the occasion, the bill for which was £43 13s. 6d.

The funds for the new structure were borrowed upon the security of mortgage of the tolls and rents of the bridge lands, which tolls and rents should have been applied to the payment of both principal and interest. Very little serious attempt was made to do more than pay the interest, and though a Sinking Fund was com-

Bridge
M. & C.

menced in 1785, tolls continued to be levied till 1903.

It cannot be doubted that the original intention in the institution of bridge-tolls was to provide a fund for the maintenance and repair of the fabric, and later on for the repayments of moneys borrowed, and not for the general enrichment of the community, and still less for private profit. It is very many years since any suggestion of irregularity under the last head has been made, but strange things happened in ancient days, as witness the proceedings of 14th February, 1400,

Rot. Pat.

when Henry IV. issued a " Commission to the Prior of Bustleham (Bisham) and John Hynden, on information that Richard Fruytour, Richard Hampteshire, William Wade and Thomas Ferrour and other men of the towns and lordships of Braye and Cokeham, Co. Berks, by pretext of letters patent of Richard II. to the bailiffs and good men of the said towns in aid of the repair of the bridge of the town of Maidenhithe have collected no small sums of money and converted the same for the most part to their own uses and not to the repair of the bridge, to enquire into the matter and summon the said Richard and other collectors and audit their account and cause the moneys collected to be applied to the repair of the bridge." In later years though the tolls were not diverted to private uses, they were constantly appropriated by the community to relieve local burdens, being regarded as part of the common fund of the town. Hence the old Bridgemasters' Accounts provide some curious reading. Subscriptions to the local races, payments of from £10 to £50 to the Mayor for his " Feast," expenses of Fifth of November celebrations, are recurring items, while there are any amount of entries for wine and beer on kings' birthdays, national victories, coronations, entertaining preachers, execution of leases, and levying fines, and indeed few were the occasions when the business, grave or gay, was not concluded without "taking something." Thus there is charged on 11th February, 1685, for a dinner at the Greyhound with " bread, beer and wine when the King was proclaimed £10 16s. 3d.," and the same day " for 2 barrells and a kilderkin of beer set in the street £1 18s. 6d." This was followed on April 23rd by a payment " at the Greyhound at the King's Coronation and for beer in the market, £2 15s. 0d." On 4th November, 1720, there was " paid for liquor taking the fines of the Quaker and Mary Field, 5s. 2d." "Expenses at the Sun on the King's birthday," on 4th June, 1772, came to £2 6s. 0d. " Jan. 8, 1779 : Paid Mr. John Clark, Mayor, for the expenses of his feast £30." Admiral Duncan's victory was celebrated on 28th October, 1797, by "beer given to 330 soldiers " costing £5 10s. 0d., while the

Maid:
I. 64, 65, 66.

Maid:
I. 65, p. 99.

Maid:
I. 65, p. 100.

Maid:
I. 65, p. 180.

Maid:
I. 66, p. 22.

Maid:
I. 64, p. 284.

Maid:
I. 66, p. 48.

death of George III. is marked by a payment to "Mr. Foster for black cloth, &c., for the pulpit and reading desk at the Chapel," amounting to £57 15s. 0d.

Maid:
I. 66. p. 172.

The legality of appropriating bridge tolls to other than bridge purposes did not pass unchallenged, notably in 1836, when Mr. John Green Bishop, having brought the question before the Town Council at a very stormy meeting, and having failed to persuade the majority to his way of thinking, published a formal protest. The practice was not, however, discontinued till matters were brought to a crisis by Mr. Joseph Taylor of Eton, in 1903.

Mr. Taylor first approached the Corporation on the subject on 6th April, 1901, and published his views on the illegality of the application of bridge funds to other than bridge purposes in pamphlet form. The Corporation, relying on ancient usage, manifested no special eagerness to alter their practice. Accordingly, Mr. Taylor, on the 21st February, 1902, lodged a petition with the Charity Commissioners, who, after some correspondence, held a public enquiry in the Town Hall on 18th November, 1902, where the Town Clerk submitted a very full memorandum on bridge matters, which, while showing that the town under its Bridge Act of 1772 had an absolute right to levy bridge-tolls, fully admitted that all surplus rents and tolls went to swell the Borough Fund and had done so ever since the bridge was built. He also showed that before Mr. Taylor came on the scene the Corporation had been for some time in communication with the Berks County Council with a view to free the bridge. By the end of the enquiry it was obvious that tolls would have to be abolished, as it was fully admitted that more than enough tolls had been received to have paid off all borrowed money long ago. Nothing was, however, done till the decision of the Charity Commissioners arrived on 13th May, 1903. But this was too long for Mr. Taylor to wait. He demanded that tolls should cease immediately, and as they were still continued, he gave public notice that "on Monday, the 8th of December," 1902, he would exercise his "right as a member of the public to pass over the Bridge in a vehicle, and to resist payment of Toll." At noon that day a remarkable scene was witnessed by a crowd of some 500 persons. Punctually to time, Mr. Taylor, with two others, was seen riding over the bridge in a motor-car. The toll-gate was closed and locked. The toll-keeper demanded toll. Mr. Taylor protested, paid, waited while the official made out a formal receipt, and then, as the great gate swung open, passed through for a few yards, and halted to address the crowd; exclaiming, as he stood in fine dramatic pose with outstretched arm, "The King's Bench will avenge the King's Highway!" a declaration which was greeted with a burst of half-ironical cheering.

The Charity Commissioners' decision was that matters could be put right only by legislation. A Bill was therefore immediately promoted by the Corporation, and in due course became law, though before it reached the Royal Assent an element of the grotesque was introduced by the further appearance on the scene of Mr. Taylor, who, with an eye to certain costs he had incurred in "avenging the King's Highway," now opposed the Bill, by which alone the bridge could be made free. In spite of this hindrance the Bill passed into law, and (*a*) abolished all tolls, (*b*) constituted bridge endowments corporate property, (*c*) required the Corporation to discharge all liabilities and arrears, and (*d*) indemnified the Corporation for previous irregularities. But even before all this was brought to full conclusion arrangements had been made to cease collecting tolls after 31st October, 1903. Once more a crowd collected at the bridge, and, as the clocks struck the hour of midnight, a great shout went up as the old gate was pulled from its hinges, carried to the top of the bridge, and thrown over into the river. It was, however, rescued next day from a watery grave, and rests now in the custody of the Borough Surveyor. The clock that stood on the toll house was at the same time removed to the Public Library. And so Maidenhead Bridge was freed.

CHAPTER III.

THE CHAPEL OF ST. ANDREW AND ST. MARY MAGDALENE.

I N an old Chronicle by a Monk of St. Chronique de la traison, &c. B. M. 2072 c. Denys who travelled in England about 1380, it is stated that "there are two bridges" at Maidenhead. The second one was that now known as the Chapel Arches, and it is highly probable that the stream running under it was much greater then than now. For it was close to this bridge that the chapel of St. Andrew was erected. In a large proportion of river-side towns and villages the church is close to the river, and this fact carries us back to days when bridges were rare or in bad condition, and when crossing a river, whether by a broken bridge, or a dangerous ford, was no light thing. Many a traveller would bow in the church, repeat a prayer, or make a vow, before he ventured the passage. It was no wonder, therefore, that the immediate vicinity of this broad and dangerous ford was the spot chosen for the church. It stood in the middle of the street, and was intended as a chapel-of-ease for the parish churches of Bray and Cookham, being on the dividing line between these two parishes, though at a Conference held in 1324, it was officially declared that henceforth it was to be deemed to be wholly in the parish of Cookham. It was erected about 1270 by (probably) some member of the Hosebund family, and certainly not by " Queen Marguerette of France, the second consort of Edward I.," as set forth in the memorial presented to George IV. in 1824. This wholly inaccurate statement was founded on the delusion that a certain royal grant of land to one Adam le Spicer in 1313, had some reference to the building of the chapel. That it could not possibly have done so is obvious from the facts that the grant is dated forty years after the chapel was erected, and the land is wholly in the parish of Bray, while the chapel was almost entirely in the parish of Cookham. As a matter of fact this land thus royally granted was in another part of the town altogether, and will claim our attention when we speak of the Town Hall, for the enlargement of which it was acquired in the reign of George II.

At the same time, as the church was erected in the middle of the street, some portion of it probably covered some amount of the road-side waste, and as this would be claimed by the Lord of the Manor, whose rights in those days were formidable as well as considerable, and as the manor belonged to the Crown, being usually part of the Queen's dowry, it is highly probable that royal consent was necessary before the building could go up, whoever built it. And as Kings were sometimes in the habit of ascribing to themselves actions which were done by their permission, though actually executed by others, this may account for the fact that in one of the Rot. Claus. Close Rolls of Ed. I., 12th June, 1293, the building is spoken of as " the King's Chapel." Further, as the Manor was part of the Queen's

INSPEXIMUS OF RICHARD II., 1393.
Confirming grant of land by Queen Margaret to Adam le Spicer.

dowry, her consent would be a necessary
formality. In 1270 the consort of Henry III.
was Queen Eleanor, and it is quite possible that
in subsequent ages some confusion arose between
her name and that of Queen Margaret, and that
to Queen Margaret was ascribed an act which
she could not possibly have performed, but which
might certainly have been done, and probably
was done, by Queen Eleanor. It may be added
also in further reference to the above quoted
expression " the King's Chapel," that in that
year, 1293, there was no Queen of England,
Edward I.'s mother having died in 1291, and
his first wife in 1290, while his second marriage
did not take place till 1299. Had there been a
queen it is quite possible the expression had been
" the Queen's Chapel." But in any case there
is no direct evidence to show that the Chapel
was a royal foundation, beyond the fact that
some part of it may have stood on land which
could only be occupied by royal consent.

Whoever built it, the church was erected
distinctly against the wishes of the Vicars of
Cookham and Bray, who saw in the new structure
promise of considerable loss to themselves, both
financial and ecclesiastical. As no proper
composition had been made with these reverend
gentlemen to secure their rights, the Bishop of
Salisbury, Walter de la Wyle, issued his prohibi- Gorham 5.
tion, placing an interdict on the building, with
the threat of greater excommunication against
any who should celebrate therein. Nevertheless
the building proceeded, though Robert de Wyke-
hampton, the succeeding bishop confirmed the

interdict on the 30th January, 1277, and Robert
Kilwardby, Primate of all England, ratified it,
and though an abortive attempt was made to
mend matters in 1310 by an Inquisition taken

by order of Bishop Simon de Ghent respecting
the site of the chapel, it was not till it had existed
for nearly fifty years that, on the application of
Roger de Mortival, bishop of Salisbury, the
ecclesiastical ban was removed in 1324 by the

Primate, Walter Reynold.

Meanwhile, not only had the building been
completed, but chaplains had been appointed,
and a chaplain's house erected. The deed of

12th June, 1293, already referred to, orders the
Keeper of Wyndelsore forest to cause Master
Ralph de Ivyngho to have in that forest six oaks
fit for timber to make a house thereof for the
use of a chaplain celebrating in the King's Chapel
of Maydenheche for the souls of the late King
Henry III. and Queen Eleanor, the King's
Mother, and Queen Eleanor the King's Consort
of the King's gift. It seems difficult to
understand how a chaplain could celebrate while
the interdict was in force, but that chaplains
were appoined during this period is certain, not

only from what is implied in the foregoing Close
Roll, but from a Patent of the same King,
Edward I., issued on 24th December, 1304,
where Theobald de Thingden is presented to the
Church at Elyndon (Elingdon or Ellington being
identified in the Calendar of Patent Rolls in the
British Museum as Maidenhead).

It has been suggested that the priest might
have been appointed to do such outside service

as the interdict did not cover, and be in readiness to execute fuller service when the prohibition was removed. This explanation, however ingenious, scarcely meets the difficulty or harmonises with canon law. A truer explanation probably is that the King on presenting knew nothing at all about the interdict. Strange as it may seem, Archbishop Walter Reynold knew nothing of it, and when asked to grant his license for its removal replied that he had searched for such an instrument in vain; which was highly probable, as Archbishop Kilwardby, on being made a Cardinal, had purloined the Registers and carried them off to Rome forty-six years before. Archbishop Reynold, however, committed the whole matter to the Bishop of Salisbury, and gave him authority to release the Maidenhead Chapel, after due investigation, from any Interdict he might discover. Gorham p. 7.

On the 25th of June, 1324, an important Conference was held in Sonning parish church, when the question of founding a perpetual chauntry in Maidenhead Chapel was discussed, and at the same time it was formally declared that the building stood in Cookham parish and not at all in Bray. The Bishop of Salisbury was represented by his Commissaries, Robert de Worth, canon of Sarum, and W. de Lullenham, rector of Hargrave. Thirteen parishioners of Cookham and nineteen of Bray had met previously and appointed William le Hosebund and William de la Rokele their proctors. William de Burton, Vicar of Cookham, appeared personally. William de Braye was proctor for both the Vicar of Bray (Henry de Chilbalton), and the Abbot of Cirencester, who was the patron of the mother churches. There were also present Nicholas de Quapplelode, Abbot of Reading, the Vicar of Sonning, and others. It was decreed that Divine Service, including the whole Mass, but excluding Sacramental offices, "may be celebrated in the Chapel of Maidenhuth for the benefit of the Inhabitants and of Travellers, without prejudice to the Mother Churches, the chapel and its Ministers being maintained entirely at the expense of the townsmen." This was episcopally confirmed the following year in a letter dated 20th June, 1325, where, however, "Baptisms of Children" were "especially forbidden." On this point the Rev. G. C. Gorham, once curate of the Chapel, to whose "Account of the Chapel" all succeeding writers on the subject must be indebted, makes the following remarks. "This prohibition has never since been removed. In very recent times, however, a Font has been introduced into the Chapel *without authority,* and baptisms are occasionally celebrated on payment of fees to the Vicar of the Parish and to the Minister, to prevent the establishment of a *right* in the inhabitants to demand the administration of the Sacrament; no Register, however, is kept at Maidenhead. The practise is clearly irregular."

The final order was made on 15th July, 1325, when the Vicar of Cookham was given the right to present annually, with the consent of the Vicar of Bray, one priest to officiate in the Chauntry of Maidenhead Chapel. Two-thirds

of all offerings were to go to the Vicar of
Cookham, and one-third to the Vicar of Bray,
except on the fair-days of St. James and St. Mary
Magdalen, when the Vicar of Cookham was to
receive the whole. The townsmen were, however, to resort on the great festivals to the Mother
Churches of Cookham and Bray, and were to
provide for the priest a dwelling-house and a
stipend of £4 per annum.

About 1352 John Hosebond, citizen and corn
dealer of London, left by will £100 for the
endowment of a "Chauntry of one Priest." This
was doubtless a new foundation, and cannot, as
Gorham supposes, have had reference to the
existing Chauntry, as the presentation to that
one was vested in the Vicar of Cookham, while
the nomination to the Hosebund foundation was
entirely in the hands of Hurley priory. The
suggestion that the rights of the Vicar of Cookham had lapsed, or were disregarded, is not a
satisfactory explanation, nor can the argument
be accepted that the existing stipend of £4 was
so small that Hosebund's gift must have been
an augmentation merely. The writer on this
point in the Victoria County History of Berkshire shows that the sum mentioned was not an
abnormally small stipend in those days. It should
be noted also, and this seems conclusive, that in
1423 there were certainly two chaplains, as they
are mentioned by name in the Salisbury record
of the institution of a hermit at Maidenhead, as
detailed above in Chapter II.

The new Chauntry was dedicated to St. Mary
Magdalene, and the double name of "Saint

V. C. H.
ii. 32.

Andrew and Saint Mary" now appears as a designation for the first time. For this Chauntry, which was for the special benefit of the souls of John Hosebond, the testator, Richard Bryde and his wife Margery, the Prior, probably Thomas

de Cumbrok (1352-1363), and Convent of Hurley were to provide a chaplain, and this they bound

themselves to do by a quadruple deed dated 1st May, 1352, where, after acknowledging the receipt of £100 from John Reyner, Hosebond's executor, they engaged " to find a fit secular chaplain to celebrate daily and to say the *placebo* with *dirige* and *commendatio,* except at Christmas, Easter, and Whitsuntide."

At the dissolution of Religious Houses, in addition to the original endowment the church was worth 13s. per annum from

(1) An acre of land called " Tryndle Acre," in a field named Wellande (or Wellhouse-field) in Cookham, given by William Brice (circ. 1500) for " a light in Maidenhead Chapel," value one shilling.

(2) House at Cookham, rent 3s. 4d.

(3) Land (not specified where) producing 4s.

(4) House and 1½ acres of land in Maidenhead value 4s. 8d. per annum (over and above 3s. 4d. paid to Eton College). It was leased by the Crown to Edward Annesley in 1570, to Margaret Annesley in 1577, and to Charles Paget in 1594. Together with No. (1) this property was granted in 1606 to Thomas Emmerson, and in the early part of the reign of Charles I. passed into the hands of John Langton, facts which had an

important bearing on a claim instituted later on
by one of the clergy of the Chapel, the Rev. John
Dawson, of whom more anon. In the reign of
Edward VI. a return dated 1548 stated that the
Chapel lands and rent were *nil*. There were
goods £2 16s. 10d., also " ij chalices, a pax, a
paire of creweths, posed (weighing) xlij oz. and
ij bells not preysed (valued)."

From 1535, when Hurley Priory was sup-
pressed and its revenues alienated to Westminster
Abbey, Maidenhead was for many years without
a chaplain. But having about 1557 elected
someone to that office, the inhabitants presented
a petition to the Crown for a grant of stipend.
Philip and Mary were then on the throne, and
the "Byll of Maydenhedd Toune to the Counsell"
then presented to them set forth with great
fulness the evil case of the people of Maidenhead.
The mother churches are " too myles or nere
thereaboutes distant " ; the people are " many
times thereof letted " from getting to them by
" vysytacyon of syckness," and floods, for
Maidenhead is low and near the river, and the
district is " dyvers times in the yere so surrounded and overflowen wyth water that your
Highness' seid subjects cannot passe goe nor
travel to their seid churches." There is no record
of any answer to this petition, but an annual
payment of seven marks (£4 13s. 4d.) has ever
since been made by the Treasury.

The appointment of a chaplain having been
taken into their own hands by the inhabitants, it
was retained by them till Elizabeth granted her
charter of Incorporation in 1582, when it passed

naturally to the Corporation, who are known to
have exercised their power at least as far back as
the earlier years of Charles I. The right to
nominate was, however, still claimed by the
inhabitants, and gave rise to protracted legal
proceedings in 1779, when the Corporation
nominated Mr. Onslow, the inhabitants Mr.
Leicester, and the Vicar of Cookham also claimed
the right to present. The Vicar early with-
drew from the contest, though there can be no
doubt that had he fought it out, to him belonged
the real right in the case. In his absence the
Corporation were adjudged victors, and they
continued patrons of the living till the Municipal
Reform Act came into force. By a grant from
Queen Anne's Bounty the chapel became a
benefice in 1726, and the first episcopal institution took place on 1st June, 1735, when the
Rev. Charles Millar was instituted by the bishop.

St. Mary's Church continued to be a " chapel
of ease," and in 1867 was placed together with
that part of the present (1931) St. Mary's parish
which lies to the north of the Bath Road in
St. Luke's parish. Maidenhead became a civil
parish on 30th July, 1870, and in 1875 St. Mary's
was constituted a parish church. It is incorrect
to speak of St. Mary's as the Parish Church of
Maidenhead; it shares that honour with All
Saints' and St. Luke's, but its long connection
with the Corporation, possibly from 1270, certainly from 1451, gives substance to its claim
to be the " Borough Church " of Maidenhead.

The Chapel has been re-built twice; at all
events there is no record of any other re-building,

and Gorham holds that the structure which was pulled down in 1724 was the original. At this time it was re-erected on the same site in the middle of the street; it provided sittings for 230 Gorham. persons, and stood for one hundred years. Old engravings picture to us a nave with rather small three sided chancel apse, with a tall round-headed window in each side. The nave windows are also shown as round-headed, while at the west end there rises a low square tower, surmounted by an open bell-turret, cupola and vane.

Of the details of its re-building we have no particulars, nor did Gorham know of any, but an old Account Book has come to light in recent years which sets forth in detail sums contributed by persons from Manchester, Oxford, Windsor, and Eton College, as well as from the locality. Who compiled the book is not known, for all the author says about himself is, "my own subscription £5 0 0." The subscriptions were collected by various ladies and gentlemen, the most prominent being Mr. Whitfield, the same doubtless as the founder of Whitfield's Charity, and of the same family as the donor of the silver plate still in use at St. Mary's Church. Mr. Darvill [*sic*], the Mayor, gave five guineas, and the familiar name of Langton stands opposite a similar amount. The chief contributor was King George I., who gave £200. The total of the receipts was £824 16s. 4d.

On the Expenses side we note such well-known names as Emblin, Meding, and Cooper, who evidently were prominent in the work, the last being specially named in connexion with stone

work. Timber came by water to Maidenhead
Bridge, and was unloaded there. Bricks cost
£6 for ten thousand. Five loads of sand cost
12/6 and a load of lime 20/-. " Spent at the
Bear on Mr. Powney and the Plasterer " is
responsible for 1/6, and perhaps it is not
uncharitable to suggest that " Money spent at
Sevll times and Places 03 :13 :6 " may also
have reference to creature comforts. Re-paint-
ing the Royal Arms cost £3 12s. 6d. The total
was £838 11s. 2d., which left a deficit of
£13 14s. 10d.

In 1824 it was deemed too small for the requirements of the town, and was also an obstruction
to traffic. Some ninety coaches were passing
through Maidenhead every day, and its
position contracted the road way to the narrow
limits of thirty-three feet. It was therefore
determined to remove the church to a more
suitable site, and this was found in its present
position, slightly to the north-west of the original
building. If of the details of the re-building
in 1724 we have no particulars, this lack is most
plentifully atoned for by the voluminous and
detailed records regarding the 1824 work.

The Architects were Messrs. Wilde and Busby
of Brighton ; the Contractor, Charles Plumridge
of Maidenhead ; the contract price was £2,860 ;
and the seating accommodation was to be for
800. A committee of management was formed
consisting of Mr. Joseph Clark (Mayor), Mr.
William Payn (Recorder), Rev. James Knollis
(Chaplain), Rev. the Hon. R. L. Melville,
Rev. Edward Neale, Mr. Charles Sawyer, Mr.

Silver
Walker.

Extracts,
p. 12.

Maid. J.
114.

Extracts
p. 17.

Jaspar Atkinson, Mr. Isaac Pocock, Mr. Richard Goolden, and the Rev. William Morgan, who acted as Secretary. They issued an appeal for funds, and set forth that the population was 2,200; that the church was too small and in the way of traffic; that the Corporation would bear the cost of the necessary Act of Parliament, but there was no rating power for building purposes; and that the outlay would be about £4,000. In response to this appeal the Corporation, in addition to bearing the cost of the Act of Parliament, gave a donation of £500, while individual members of that body subscribed from £10 to fifty guineas a piece. A memorial was also presented to George IV., in which the old fiction of a "royal foundation" was again made to do duty. It evidently served its purpose as the response was a donation of £200. The stone-laying was a brilliant function. It took place on 22nd July, 1824, and the Borough records set forth in great detail how the Corporation walked in procession, headed by the Corporation School, "newly clothed," how the mayor performed the ceremony, and how a casket containing coins of the realm was duly deposited. Then the building proceeded. So did a lively dispute between the Corporation and the Chaplain as to the latter's stipend, and especially how much was fairly due to him in lieu of certain pew rents. The dispute was still unsettled when the new chapel was ready for use, which will probably account for the fact that there was no ceremonial opening, but that on Sunday, 9th October, 1825, divine service was held for the first time in the

Extracts, p. 20.

Maid. R. 190.

Extracts 22.

new building without any special function to mark the occasion. The difference between the Corporation and the Chaplain was laid before the Commissioners for Building Churches, and was at length settled. Preserved in the Borough Deed Box is a document setting forth that the Rev. James Knollis, the Chaplain, is to receive £62 7s. 0d. out of the pew rents of the Free Chapel at Maidenhead.

Maid. J. 115.

The Chapel was adorned with some stained glass of superior quality. Alas, it all disappeared at the time of a subsequent alteration. Where it went or who had it, are amongst those things which are hidden from all men. On the score of truth its loss is scarcely to be deplored. It celebrated the benefactions of four royal personages, not one of whom had conferred any benefit on the church, and by a singular perversity it omitted all reference to four other royal personages who had been real benefactors. It is not true that Queen Margaret "dedicavit," that either Richard II., or Henry VI. "confirm't" or that Elizabeth "restituit," though all these fictions were blazoned forth with much heraldry and gorgeous colour in the East Window. It had been far more to the point to have commemorated Queen Mary, who granted the Minister a pension; Queen Anne, whose bounty augmented the stipend; George I., who gave £200 to the building fund of 1724; and George IV., who gave a similar sum one hundred years later. The west window displayed three shields. One bore a Virgin's head with the legend "Maydenheth" in allusion to the fanciful

Gorham.

derivation of the name of the town; another set forth the device of the borough seal; and the third bore a head of Saint Andrew with the legend, "Sanctus Andreas Patronus."

The organ was the gift of Lady Pocock, Maid. R. 190. having been presented by her to the former Chapel on 29th April, 1817, and an altar-piece of no little artistic merit was painted for, and presented to, the church in 1825 by that versatile genius, Isaac Pocock, who, having gained dis- Dic. Nat. Biog. tinction with his brush, achieved further victories with his pen, especially as a dramatist. Several of his plays had considerable success. They were written chiefly at Maidenhead, where he settled after inheriting some property from his uncle, Sir Isaac Pocock, the husband of the donor of the organ.

The Communion Plate is from several hands. Two silver flagons, a chalice, and a paten are each inscribed "Ricardus Robinson, Civis Londinensis dedit in usum Capellæ de Maidenhead natus ibidem 1657" (Richard Robinson, citizen of London, gave it for the use of the Chapel of Maidenhead, his native place). A silver plate bears the inscription "D. D. J. Whitfield Ar. in Usum Capellæ De Maidenhead pro Pane consecrato, Ano. Dom. 1727" (J. Whitfield, Esq., gave it for the use of the Chapel of Maidenhead for the consecrated bread). A chalice, paten, and silver spoon were given in 1838, the chalice being inscribed, "Presented to St. Mary's Chapel, Maidenhead, on Christmas Day, 1838, for the consecrated Wine, by J. Knollis, B.D., the Chaplain,

G. C. Gorham, B.D., the Curate, and 70
persons in the Congregation."

Three Mural tablets, removed from the old
church, commemorate John Whitfield, d. 9 Ap.,
1663, David Gregory, M.D., Savilian Professor
of Astronomy at Oxford, d. 1720, and Robert
Bever, d. 29 April, 1723, Under Sheriffe of
Berks and Mayor of Maidenhead. Other tablets
preserve the memory of James Payne, Maidenhead's celebrated Recorder, d. 1822, and the
Rev. Thomas Lingwood, d. 1872, for ten years
incumbent of this Church.

Gorham, 30.   By an agreement made in 1334 between the
Bishop of Salisbury and William Rokele and
William Housebond, proctors for Maidenhead,
provision had been made for a dwelling-house for
the Chaplain. It was probably the same as that
specified in a deed of 1412 (now lost), whereby
Gorham.   John Cook (heir of Housebond) enfeoffs certain
inhabitants of a " messuage with a small croft
of land and fish-pooles near the chapell for the
Chaplein ther." It was called the Priest House,
or Town House, and is described in the deed of
22nd August : 23 Henry VIII. (lost) as lying
" between the tenement of Thomas Annesley
called Fotter's on the West and the several
waters of Thomas Annesley called Le Broke on
the East." It was on the north of the main
street, opposite the ancient chapel, and adjoining the east side of the present iron-gates of
the Chapel yard, and part of the present garden
is identical with that mentioned in the grant of
1412. In 1531 it was in the hands of Henry
Annesley, who allowed the profits to go to

the repair of Maidenhead Bridge. Annesley exchanged it for Devenysh House, an ancient mansion standing on the site of the present vicarage, enfeoffing certain inhabitants of the town "for the sole use and maintenance of Maidenhead Bridge." How the profits of the Priest House, which had thus been deflected to the Bridge, came back to their original pious uses is not known, but about 1557 the Priest House was "very ruinous and decayed," and it was rebuilt by the Corporation as a residence for the Chaplain, but the land originally granted with it was not re-annexed.

Two hundred years later, in 1753, the Priest House was exchanged with the Corporation for ground on which Devenyshe House formerly stood, and on that land the present vicarage was erected. Copped Hall, which formerly stood on the site of the Market House, had recently been bought and pulled down by the Corporation, who gave its timbers to help in the construction of the new parsonage. The Corporation also gave £150 in money, and the then Chaplain, the Rev. Humfrey Henchman, was also a liberal benefactor to the extent of "many hundred pounds."

Maid. B. 190, p. 26.

CHAPTER IV.

THE CHAPLAINS.

Kerry, 138. NO complete list of the Chaplains or Incumbents of this Church has ever been compiled, and the Salisbury Registers contain no entry prior to 1735. The following list, though by no means exhaustive, is the most complete that has yet been published :—

Rot. Pat. Robert de Harwedon. Resigned in 1304.

Rot. Pat. Theobald de Thingden, 1304. Presentation made by the Crown by reason of voidance of the See of Winchester.

Cookham C. R. Galfridus. Circ. 1395.

Maid. O. 157. Blower. Circ. 1412. Name in deed of feoffment of Chaplain's house 18th March, 13 Hen : IV., produced in Dawson v. Corporation in 1637 (now missing) and quoted in "Instructions to Counsel" with marginal note "Capelli Blower then livg [living]."

Sarum Epis Reg. Chandler, fol. 40, 41. John Coter and Robert Circ. 1423. These two names occur in an admission of a Hermit to Maidenhead Hermitage, 29th October, 1423.

Thomas Mettingham. Circ. 1452.	First Overseer of the Guild of Maidenhead.	Rot. Pat.
Thomas Bayly. Circ. 1536.	Stipend paid to Thomas Bayly, Clerk, Curate Maydenhead belonging to the late priory of Hurley for one year, allowed this year as last £4 13 4.	Land Revenue Receipts A/c. 34 Hen. VIII. [1542-3]. Bundle 95, No. 7. See B.B.O., vol. 15, p. iii.
Henry Wood. Circ. 1579.	Name in Will of John Webb of Maidenhead, 1579, in Court of Archd. of Berks, Oxford.	Kerry, 138.
James Spigurnell. Circ. 1606.	Died circ. 1630.	C. C. R.
John Dawson, 1630-1641.	(See below.)	Gorham, 37.
Sampson Bond. Circ. 1646.	Sermon preached before the Committee of Divines and published by order 1646.	
Matthew Hole.		Gorham, 38.
Christopher Newstead, 1650.	(See below.)	Cal. St. Pap. Dom.
John Jones, 1670.		Kerry, 138.
John Lord, 1672.	(See below.)	Maid. R. 189, p. 257.
John Thompson, 1681.	Was still Chaplain in 1728.	Gorham, 39.
Charles Millar, 1st June, 1735.	First Chaplain to receive institution from the Bishop.	Gorham, 39.
Humfrey Henchman, 30th June, 1743.	The present vicarage was built in his time, and largely through his liberality.	Gorham, 39.

Salisbury Instit. Reg.	Arthur Onslow, 1st March, 1782.	Son of General Onslow, and nephew to the Speaker; Dean of Worcester and Archdeacon of Berks. Died 1817.
Maid, R. 190, p. 421.	Henry Dodwell.	Elected 24th Oct., 1817, but could not accept. His long and appreciative letter declining is copied in full in Maid. R. 190.
Maid, R. 190, p. 423. Salisbury Instit. Reg.	John Greig, 2nd May, 1818.	Elected 24th Nov., 1817.
Maid. R. 190, p. 434. Salisbury Instit. Reg.	James Knollis, 13th Sep., 1819.	Elected 26th July, 1819.
Oxf. Dioc. Reg.	Edward Owen, 29th Aug., 1860.	
Oxf. Dioc. Reg.	Thomas J. Lingwood, 20th Feb., 1862.	
Oxf. Dioc. Reg.	Thomas N. Kearney, D.D., 1873.	
Oxf. Dioc. Reg.	William A. Hill, March 1881.	
Oxf. Dioc. Reg.	Charles Hewitson Nash, 31st May, 1893.	
	Cecil H. Clissold, 27 Sep., 1928.	

Of the foregoing, the Rev. JOHN DAWSON, who was born at Oxford about 1605, was one of the most remarkable. His chaplaincy lasted from 1630 to 1641. Charles I. had been five years on the throne when Dawson came to Maidenhead. He was chaplain through all those years of stress and excitement that culminated

in the great Civil War. Strafford and Laud and
Pym and Hampden were names of everyday
mention to him, and he himself was as restless
as the times. At least the Corporation thought Wood's Athenæ Oxonienses.
so; for while he was reputed as a most eminent
preacher and was much resorted to, the towns-
people called him " a restless spirit, and an Gorham.
unreasonable man." He was evidently a gentleman who had a lively idea of his rights, and he
had not long been in Maidenhead before he began
to claim them. Matters came to such a pass
that one day (1633-4) scarcely had he ceased
officiating in the church, or had got very far
from the building when an " arrest " was made Cal. St. Pap. Dom. Jan. 30, 1639.
upon him, though for what specific cause is not
stated. The quarrel having been laid before the
proper authority, Archbishop Laud and the
Lord Keeper were appointed referees in the Cal. St. Pap. Dom. 23 June, 1634.
matter. On 23rd June, 1634, they reported
that they directed Bishop Bancroft of Oxford
and Dr. Charles Tooker to repair to Maidenhead
and investigate, which they did, and, as they
fondly imagined, settled everything. The town
promised to pay Mr. Dawson all arrears of
salary; to give him 4d. weekly for every scholar
learning English only, and 6d. for such as
learned to write or cypher, instead of 3d. and
4d. as formerly; to give him £5 for dilapida-
tions, and " 10s. towards the repair of an old
hovel in his back yard." But scarcely had the
Bishop left when the Chaplain set up a new
claim. The town resisted, and negotiations
were broken off.

The new claim was threefold. First, he

disputed the right of the Corporation to the Priest House with its land; secondly, he disputed their right to an adjacent house and land called Devenysh; and lastly he claimed Trindle Acre in or near Cookham. The "Instructions to Counsel" in this case are still in existence, and are carefully preserved in the Borough Deed Chest, being calendared as O 157. They show that the Corporation's title to the Priest House was derived from John Cook, the heir of Hosebund, as stated above, and dated from the reign of Henry IV., while Devenysh House had been granted in the reign of Henry VIII. by Henry Annesley to Silvester Peck and others for the benefit of the town, and the Corporation had repeatedly made leases respecting it. Four of these documents are still in existence. One, dated 12th February, 1611-12, is the oldest known document bearing the Borough Seal, and all four of them reserve to the Corporation the "free use of the haul, buttory, Kitchyn, and all other roomes needful," for ten days, to hold there "some help-ale" for the benefit of the chapel. These "help-ales" or Whitsun-Ales, as they were often called, from the season when they were generally held, were by no means unusual methods of assisting Church funds before bazaars and "sales of work" were invented. Dancing, archery, sports, not always the most refined, and the consumption of any amount of liquor filled up the time, and filled up the coffers.

It is interesting to note that in 1633, while the dispute between Mr. Dawson and the town

Maid.
O. 157.

Maid.
H. 61.

was pending, the latter granted a lease of
Devenysh House to one, John Frize, and in this
document no mention is made of any profit from
any Whitsun Ale going to the Chapel.

Gorham, 32.

Mr. Dawson's third claim in respect of Trindle
Acre brought Mr. John Langton on the scene,
who produced a deed of 6th October, 1606, and,
tracing possession through Thomas Emerson
and Wm. Bennett to Wm. Paget and then to
Gervase Vronston and lastly to himself, showed
conclusively that he was the rightful owner.
The claim of the Corporation was enforced by
the production of several deeds, now lost, but
which are set forth in an old minute book under
the dates of 3rd May and 26th September, 1637,
when, by order of the Court of Chancery,
Thomas Davys, the Warden, produced the
following documents :—

Maid. R. 189, 33, 34.

1 May, 26 Ed : III. Quadruple deed by Prior
of Hurley.

25 Mar : 1334. Act by Bishop of Salisbury.

28 Mar : [13] Hen : IV. Deed by John Cook.

22 Aug : 23 Hen : VIII. Henry Annesley to
the town. Sale of Devenysh House.

14 Feb : 23 : Hen : VIII. Ditto. Feofment
of Devenysh.

An attempt was made to settle these differences
in camera, and Gorham states that "an original
letter still exists, from Sir Henry [Marks,
Attorney General] to the Warden of Maidenhead, appointing 1st July, 1635, for hearing
both parties at his house in Aldersgate Street.
The attempt failed, and the case came into court,
when the combined effect of all the foregoing

Gorham, 38.

evidence was that the Reverend Mr. Dawson lost the day hopelessly. The final order of Archbishop Laud and the Lord Keeper bears date

30th January, 1638-9. The referees compliment the Bishop of Oxford and Dr. Tooker upon the pains they had taken, and strongly censure the Chaplain for " his causeless trouble " given to the town. He is ordered " to acknowledge his fault in not conforming " to what the Bishop and Dr. Tooker had settled ; he is " to conform thereto in all points" ; and if he again "presume to trouble His Majesty or the Board any more on this business," he shall be " committed to the Fleet." And as for that " arrest " the men of Maidenhead made on the Chaplain, "although the inhabitants were much to be blamed for suffering it to be done so near the Chapel, and upon a day when he had been reading divine service, yet in regard it is five years since, it was ordered that they should not be further troubled by Dawson concerning that particular."

So ended a memorable contest. John Dawson died in September, 1641, aged about 36 years, and rests in Cookham churchyard. Peace to his memory, for there was not much peace about him while he was living.

CHRISTOPHER NEWSTED was born in 1597, and after leaving the University had the advantage of foreign travel, accompanying Sir Thomas Roe on his embassy to Turkey. Returning to England, he settled in Abingdon, being from 19th June, 1629, to 1640, vicar of St. Helen's. In 1642 Archbishop Laud nominated him to Stisted in Essex, but the nomination was not confirmed by the lords, and his presentation was delayed till 23rd May, 1643. But by this time rumour had been busy. Strange reports got abroad, and when Newsted arrived at Stisted, so warm, not to say hot, was his welcome that he could not obtain possession of his rectory, and it is more than doubtful if he ever entered inside his church at all.

In 1644 (or according to others, July, 1645) he was sequestered by the Earl of Manchester, but the " Committee for Plundered Ministers," in pity for his wife, granted her one-fifth of the rectory profits, and in 1650 the same Committee appointed him to Maidenhead, the " Committee for Maintenance of Ministers " granting him at the same time an augmentation of £50. But the " Committee of Approbation of Public Preachers " demurred on the ground of the previous sequestration, and Messrs. Nye, Lockyer and Sterry were deputed to enquire " as to his submission to the present Government, and fitness to preach." Newsted at once petitioned for continuance of his augmentation and for ecclesiastical status. The position was referred to Major-General Goffe, and his certificate thereon was in its turn referred to Messrs. Lockier, Bunkley and Oxenbridge, to report whether Newsted ought to be allowed to preach. Later on, in August, 1657, the whole matter was laid before four other Commissioners who were " to speak with Newsted, and certify as to his fitness to be restored to his ministrations." At the restoration he petitioned for the profits of Stisted Rectory, and though unsuccess-

Cal. St. Pap. Dom. Feb. 7, 1654-5.

Cal. St. Pap. Dom.

ful in this, he gained the same year, on 25th
August, 1660, a prebendal stall in St. Paul's
Cathedral, a preferment which he continued to
hold till his death in 1662. He was the author
of a work entitled "An Apology for Women,
or Women's Defence." He was 23 when he
wrote it.

JOHN LORD was by the Corporation elected
Minister and Chaplain on 13th August, 1672,
and in due course entered on his duties. Four
years later he was cited to Salisbury to show
by what authority he officiated at Maidenhead.
Whether his Salisbury experience had a dis-
couraging effect on him, or no, his ministrations
grew lax, and the Corporation resolved to get
rid of him. On 16th January, 1680-1, they
formally resolved "that Mr. John Lord Minister
of this Corporation hath neglected to officiate at
his Duty in this place as he ought to have done
and as the Ecclesiasticall and Cannon Lawes of
the Church doe require It is therefore hereby
Ordered and Declared that the Election of the
said Mr. Lord formerly made is now null and
void And that Care be taken that another
Minister bee obtained and gotten to Officiate in
the said Chappell in place and stead of the said
Mr. John Lord And that the keys of the said
Chappell and of the house belonging to the said
Minister together wh the possion of the said
Chappell and house be delivered forthwith unto
the Warden and Bridgemasters or either of
them."

The proceedings were, of course, entirely

Maid. R. 189.
p. 257.

Gorham.

Maid. R. 189.
p. 267.

illegal and *ultra vires,* but when did a trifle like
that frighten the men of Maidenhead?

Although GEORGE CORNELIUS GORHAM Dic. Nat.
Biog.
was only a curate whilst resident in Maidenhead, and though his period of service at
St. Mary's was less than three years, it is
impossible to pass over a name which a few
years afterwards became a household word in
the Church of England, as the result of his
controversies with Bishop Phillpots of Exeter
as to the true Anglican position on baptismal
regeneration. Born in 1787, the son of a banker
in Huntingdonshire, and educated under Quaker
influences, he graduated at Cambridge, coming
out third wrangler in 1808. Already his views
on baptismal regeneration were not sufficiently
high to please the powers of the day, and in 1811
Dr. Dampier, Bishop of Ely, threatened to with-
hold consent to ordination. Gorham, however,
manifested his characteristic firmness and the
Bishop gave way.

To theology Gorham had added the studies of
archæology and botany, his herbareum being
subsequently sold for a considerable sum, while
amongst his archæological writings is the
scholarly and full " Account of the Chapel of
Saint Andrew and Saint Mary Magdalene at
Maidenhead," to which the present writer has
already acknowledged his indebtedness.

Amongst the preferments he held were the
curacy of Clapham from 1818 to 1827; the curacy
of Maidenhead from 1840 to 1842; St. Just-in-
Penwith, Cornwall, to which he was presented
by Lord Lyndhurst; and Brampford Speke,

near Exeter, on the presentation of Lord Chancellor Cottenham. Here it was he crossed swords with Bishop Phillpots, who refused to institute him till after examination. The Bishop found Gorham a harder nut to crack than he had expected, in spite of the " intricate, perplexing, and difficult questions " with which he "endeavoured to implicate him." But as Gorham repudiated the doctrine that regeneration is in all cases the accompaniment of baptism, the Bishop refused to institute. The Court of Arches decided against Gorham on the ground that Baptismal Regeneration is the doctrine of the Church of England. The Judicial Committee of the Privy Council reversed this decision, on the ground that a difference of opinion on this point had existed among English Churchmen from the Reformation onward. In vain did the Bishop appeal to the Queen's Bench, the Common Pleas, and the Exchequer; each court in turn decided against him. Gorham was instituted, and a silver tea service and a purse of money indicated a large measure of public sympathy. Gorham's pen was responsible for over fifty works, to say nothing of the veritable library that sprang into being as the result of his battles in the Law Courts. He died in 1857.

Benham's Dic. Relig.

CHAPTER V.

THE CORPORATION AND THE CHARTERS.

HE Corporation of Maidenhead is the lineal descendant of the Guild of St. Andrew and St. Mary Magdalen, founded in the reign of Henry VI. At that time Thomas Mettingham was priest Rot. Pat. 30 Hen. VI. p. 2, m. 1. of John Hosebund's Chauntry in Maidenhead Chapel, and he it was whose petition laid the foundation of Maidenhead's corporate life. In response to his appeal the King issued his Letters Patent dated 20th Dec: 30 Hen: VI (1451) authorising the formation of a Guild, to be called "The Overseer, Wardens, Brethren, and Sisters of the Fraternity or Guild of St. Andrew and St. Mary Magdalene, of Maidenhuth." Such guilds were common all over England. Their original purpose was to serve the common weal, and in some respects they were analogous to modern Friendly Societies. To these succeeded the religious guilds for the performance of works of mercy and religious rites. Some seem to have combined both ideas, and of such was the one at Maidenhead. It was charged with the "perpetual maintenance and confirmation of the aforesaid Chauntry," the finding of wax lights and other articles necessary for the celebration of masses, and the "continual reparation and keeping up of the bridge over the Thames."

The first members of the Guild were :—
Thomas Mettingham, the chaplain; John Noris,
esquire of the body to Hen : VI.; John Pury,
esquire; William Noris; Roger Noris; Thomas
Babham; and Henry Fraunceis. They were
empowered to elect other brethren and sisters,
to elect annually two wardens, to make rules for
the Guild, and to have a common seal. Thomas
Mettingham was to be Overseer, and his successors in the chauntry were to succeed to that
office also.

Such being the origin of Maidenhead's
corporate life, it is evident that those writers
are in error who for the last two hundred years
in Gazetteers, Guidebooks and Directories have
re-iterated the fiction that Maidenhead's first
Charter came from Edward III. on 1st May,
1352. The mistake arises from supposing a
quadruple deed of that date to have been a
charter of incorporation. It was nothing of the
kind; it was the deed wherein the Prior and
Convent of Hurley bound themselves in a sum
of £100 to find a priest for the chantry newly
founded by John Hosebund as set forth in a
previous chapter. Beyond the fact that the deed
is calendared with the Close Rolls of Edward
III., that King had nothing to do with it.

Like all similar institutions, the Maidenhead
guild was dissolved in 1547, and however much
of good may have accrued to religion by the
suppression of religious houses, the sweeping
away of the guilds struck a lamentable blow at
corporate life in England. Application was,
however, made to Queen Elizabeth for a re-estab-

lishment of a guild or corporation. The
petitioners were Sir Henry Neville, William
Weldon, Silvester Peck, Robert Davus and
John Webb. The result was the Inspeximus
bearing date 18th Aug : 20 Eliz : (1578), which _{Maid.} _{Char.} I.
is the earliest of the charters or corporate letters
patent preserved by the Borough, the original
deed of Henry VI. being in the custody of the
Record Office. It was followed soon after by
Maidenhead's first Charter of Incorporation
dated 7th March 24 Eliz : (1581-2). By it _{Maid.} _{Char.}
Maidenhead became a Free Town and its
inhabitants a body corporate under the name of
" The Warden, Bridge Masters, Burgesses, and
Commonalty of the Town of Maydenheth." The
Corporation succeeded to all the duties of the
ancient guild except that of superintending and
maintaining the divine offices in the chapel.
The connexion between the chapel and the
corporation was, however, very close, and was
maintained till the Municipal Reform Act of _{Gorham.}
1835. Patronage passed into the hands of the
Corporation, the care of the fabric devolved upon
them, they expended considerable sums of
money on the rebuilding, the Bridgemasters _{Maid. O. 159,}
officiated as Churchwardens, and seats in the _{Municip. Corp. Rep.}
chapel were allotted not only to all the officers _{Maid. O. 158.}
and members of the Corporation but also to
their families.

Upon the Bridgemasters also fell the duty of
entertaining the visiting ministers and clergy
who from time to time came from a distance to
do duty, and their account books show how well

they understood the rites of hospitality. For example :—

Maid. I. 65, p. 16.

1665. July 16. Paid for wine to present
the minister that preached ... 3   o

p. 40.

1671. Paid Mr. Cleere for preaching ... 7   6

Paid at the same time 1   6

p. 64.

1678. Pd. at the Greyhound when Mr.
Nash preached 4   8

Pd. for 2 lbs. Sack when Mr.
Bassett preached 4   o

Paid at the Bull when Mr. Jones
preached 4   4

Pd. at the Saracen's Head for a
stranger that preached ... 10   o

These last four entries, be it noted, follow on in the original as shown.

By this Charter provision was made for a scale of tolls for merchandise passing over the bridge, a market was to be held every Monday, fairs on the Feasts of St. Mary Magdalen and Saint Andrew, and a Court of Pie Powder was established of which something must be said later in the Chapter on " Courts."

Maid. Char. 3.

The next Charter was granted by James I. on 4th August, 1604. It bears evidence of progress. Maidenhead is evidently increasing in importance—its Warden is to have two Mace-bearers to carry silver or gilt maces before him ; and in commerce—it is to have an additional fair on Whit Wednesday. Three trees also are granted yearly from Cookham Woods for the repair of the bridge. The other provisions of Elizabeth's Charter are confirmed.

From the reports of Sir Edward Palmer,

Attorney General in the reign of Charles II., B. B. O. Vol. 13, No. 1, p. 23. printed in 1678, it would seem that this grant of King James did not pass wholly unchallenged, for in the 17th year of his reign there was an action of Quo Warranto brought against the Corporation to show by what right Maidenhead held its markets and collected its dues. The case was argued out on highly technical points, and though some of the most important of these were given against the town, it was reported that " no judgment was given for the King in this case, but that the Corporation will enjoy the privileges, notwithstanding this action." Why it was brought at all, or who originated it, are mysteries. It has been suggested that perhaps some person who objected to tolls—there have been such persons—thought he saw a flaw in the title, and attacked it accordingly.

Maidenhead having by these charters become a Free Town, its inhabitants were allowed to become Free Men, a position highly valued in those days, and for long years afterwards highly cherished and jealously guarded. Persons were only admitted to the freedom by vote of the Corporation on taking the freeman's Oath, and on payment of a considerable fine, unless the same was remitted because the applicant was the son of a freeman, or for some other sufficient reason. It is curious to note that the very earliest corporate minute now in existence relates Maid. R. 189, p. 33. to the admission of a free man, one Nicholas Widmore, a tanner, who was admitted on 27th July, 1636. " Memorandum qd. vicessimo septimo die Julii anno regni d̄m nos Caroli Regis

Dei grat Angliæ Scotiæ ffranciæ et Hibīne &c.
duodecimo 1636 Nichus Widmore tanner
admissus est per redemptionem in lībtatem
hujus Guild et solvit de fine ad usum communis
villæ Vo' et pstit sacramt qd. bene et fideliter
observabit omnes legales ordines et consuitu-
dines ejusdem villæ Tempore Thome Davys
guardiani et Johis Langton & Willmi Weskott
pontinarios item.''

Maid. R.
189, p. 35.
It would seem that sometimes the status of a
free man was conferred only after probation.
Thus on 24th October, 1638, it was ordered that
Thomas Smith of Thame shall exercise his trade
of a locksmith for six months only, ''and if then
he shall be well liked and approved of he shall
then put in good security to the parish for
saving harmless the said parish, and shall then
pay for his redemption for his fine £5 to the
use of the common chest.''

Maid.
R. 190.
For at least another hundred years a like
vigilance was exercised, as on 17th January,
1728, William Childe, having traded as a wheel-
wright without the permission of the Corporation,
is ordered to forbear using his trade under a
penalty of forty shillings a month.

Maid.
Q. 188.
The list of freemen was preserved with more
or less care down to 1831, and was periodically
and officially examined. The volume closes with
a final certificate of inspection dated 4th August,
1834.

Although freemen in the old sense of the word
were now no more, the Legislature saw in the
title a method whereby municipalities could
confer distinction on such as they might desire

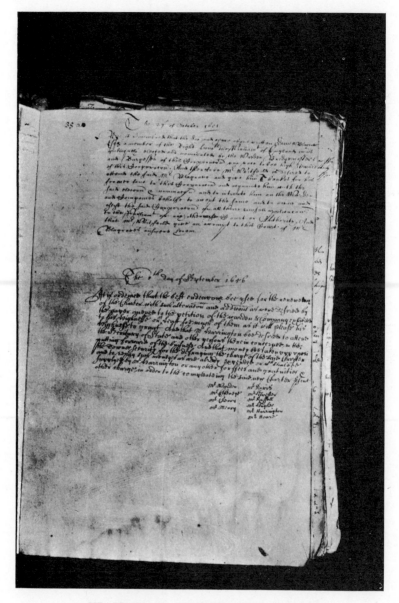

(1) MR. BLAGRAVE APPOINTED HIGH STEWARD.
(2) APPLICATION TO CROMWELL FOR A CHARTER.

to honour, and at the same time link on the present with the past. An Act was passed giving corporations power to elect Honorary Freemen. The position, which is entirely honorary, and carries with it no privileges, has been conferred by Maidenhead on Alderman Cox (the then Mayor) and Lord Desborough, the High Steward, in 1918, and on Alderman J. W. Walker in 1928.

During the protectorate application was made to Cromwell for a new charter. A list of alterations and emendations was drawn up and attached to a petition, which, on 8th September, 1656, by solemn resolution of the Corporation, was confided to the care of a Mr. Harrington, who was to wait on the Secretary of State and others and forward the business, obtaining the alterations the town desired, " or soe much of them as it will please his Highness to grant."

Maid. R. 189, p. 35a.

No charter was, however, obtained at that time, the next one being from the hand of Charles II., on 12th March 15 Ch : II. (1662-3). This document simply confirmed what had gone before with one alteration, market-day was changed from Monday to Wednesday. This was, however, evidently considered a great gain, as a lease of the bridge tolls was on the 1st of March of the following year granted to William Cherry of Maidenhead, " for and in consideration of the great charge and expense that the said William Cherry hath been att in renewing the Charter of the said Town and in altering the Market day of the same Towne which is likely to prove very advantageous."

Maid. Ch. 4.

Maid. J. 83.

Maid.
Ch. 5.

Maid. R. 189,
p. 52.

The last Charter was granted on 15th June, 1685, by James II. It was obtained as the result of petition, the same being resolved upon by the Corporation on 9th June, 1684, " upon good considerations and weighty reasons." The usual practice seems to have been followed. The whole of the " rights, liberties and privileges " of the town, together with the existing charter, were surrendered into the King's hands for him to re-grant the same with such " additions and alterations as His Majesty shall in his Kingly wisdom think fit." The " Kingly wisdom " accordingly confirmed the previous Charter, raised the Warden to the rank of Mayor, appointed a High Steward, and also a Steward who should act as Town Clerk.

No further change took place till the advent of the Municipal Reform Act, when the future government of the town was confided to a Mayor, four Aldermen, and twelve Councillors, the first mayoral election under the new regime taking

Municip.
Corp. Rep.

place on 1st January, 1836. It is interesting to note that in the Report of the Commissioners which preceded the passing the Municipal Reform Bill, it was recorded that the Corporation was "popular," and its individual members " generally respected."

Up to this time few, if any, of the Corporation had been nonconformists. The Corporation Act which received the royal assent of Charles II. in 1661 provided that no person should be elected to office in any corporate town who should not within one year previously have taken the Sacrament of the Lord's Supper according to the rites of the Church of England. The Act of 1673 extended this requirement to magistrates, and the Act of 1685 to all public officers, civil and military. These enactments were after a time suspended by temporary statutes, but it was not till 1828 that they were finally abolished. The Bridgemasters' accounts contain many items of expense for journeys to Cookham Church " to qualify," and preserved among the Borough muniments are a large number of parchment certificates setting forth that A. B. attended and received the Sacrament of the Lord's Supper on taking office as Mayor, Maid.
A. 23. magistrate, excise-officer, or what not. The latest of these certificates is dated 4 Jan : 1807.

It has sometimes been a matter for regret in modern times that prominent citizens who by position, education, and business aptitude, were well qualified for municipal office, have shrunk from bearing that burden, but there has never been a lack of candidates, and one is at a loss to understand the apparently widespread reluctance to serve on the Council in pre-reform days. Several entries in the minute books bear witness to this, of which the following may serve Maid.
R. 190. as an example. On 7th February, 1745-6, it was ordered that those persons who refused to take the office of Burgess after being duly elected, should in future pay a fine of £10 instead of £5 as formerly, as " it appears there is a combination in the said town rather to pay the said sum of £5 than to take on them the said office of Burgess, which tends to the subversion of the Government of the said town."

R. 190.
pp. 343, 349.
365.

The year 1804-5 witnessed a very exceptional event, nothing less in fact than the expulsion from the Corporation of Mr. Abraham Darby, a prominent citizen, one of the Burgesses, and a former Mayor. The reason given in the minute of 3 September, 1804, was that Mr. Darby had left the town, but the vigour with which that gentleman took up the matter suggests that there were other reasons which are not recorded. Anyhow, Mr. Darby applied for, and obtained a Mandamus, calling on the Corporation to say why he should not be re-instated. And re-instated he was. The Mandamus was read at a Council Meeting on 5 May, 1805, and Mr. Darby was restored to his office, continuing a member of the Corporation till 4 May, 1811, when he voluntarily resigned.

Minute Books are decorous documents, and usually confine themselves to recording results rather than the processes by which they were arrived at. Doubtless, however, there were stirring scenes in the days of the old Corporation, as there have sometimes been in the new, but the humour of the situation has not often surpassed an incident which took place between 1840-50. So sharply divided were the two parties on the Council that on the 9th November, when they entered the Hall to choose the Mayor, not only would they not speak to each other, but one party retired to the end of the room to get as far away from their rivals as possible. These latter at once saw their opportunity, and no sooner had the clock struck twelve, than someone immediately proposed, someone else seconded, and there was forthwith elected one of themselves as Mayor. When at length the others returned to the table and enquired when business would begin, they learned to their chagrin that it had already begun, and the most important item was settled.

For many years it was customary for the Mayor, or Warden, to give a " feast " on his election to office, a breakfast on the day when his successor was chosen, and another breakfast on the day he relinquished office and his successor was sworn in. In 1709 it was thought this was asking too much of the town's chief Officer, and it was resolved that " the Mayor and company shall breakfast with the old Mayor on the day of election, and the old Mayor is to be excused the breakfast on the day the Mayor is sworn." The whole expense of the " feast " did not fall on the Mayor (or Warden), varying sums being voted for the purpose from the town funds, as numerous entries in the Bridgemasters' accounts testify. Prior to 1644 twenty nobles or £6 13s. 4d. was the sum allowed, but it was then discontinued for ten years in consequence of the distressing Civil War at that time raging. On its resumption later the amount spent from public funds varied from £10 to £50. As a regular function it ceased in 1815. In passing, it may be noted that if in the " good old days " feasts were substantial things, so too were fasts. In 1755 a royal proclamation set aside February 6th as a solemn fast day, and it was " ordered that no person shall keep open shop or ale house from 10 to 5."

Maid. R. 189, p. 73.

Maid. R. 189, p. 30a.

Maid. R. 190.

Maid. R. 194.

The Mayor's feast was not the only occasion which the good men of Maidenhead found for conviviality. Maidenhead was a loyal town, and royal birthdays seemed peculiarly suitable for practising the rites of hospitality. On one of these occasions one of the company, overcome with " hospitality," so far forgot himself as to " go for " His Worship the Mayor and strike him. An assault on the King himself could hardly have excited greater astonishment and indignation, and what to do with a miscreant guilty of such an outrage no one knew. Happily for the honour of the town there were no precedents for such a case, and we are willing to believe that there has been nothing like it since. The record on the Corporation minutes is very full, but it is too unique to be curtailed.

R. 189.
p. 57.

"Memorandum. That on the 30 day of October Anno Domini 1732 the Worshipful the Mayor and Burgesses Clergy Gentry of the said Corporation assembled in the most loyal manner to drink their Majesties and Royal Families' health in a public manner there being present divers military officers with their soldiers who in regard to the day in great loyalty discharged their guns after drinking the said healths. When John Kimber the younger of the said town, barber, in a most insolent manner affronted quarrelled with and struck the Mayor and Company. The like actions being never remembered or heard of to be done before in the said Corporation by any person whatsoever, on mature consideration for a punishment for the said offence divers severe punishments was [sic] thought on which might have ended in the ruin of himself and family of which the Corporation was compassionate and tender. And at last gave sentence that he should ask the Mayor and Company's pardon in the public market Place in the most submissive manner in the following words, viz. :—

"Whereas I, John Kimber, did on Monday night last (being the King's birthday) assault and strike the Worshipful the Mayor of this corporation to the hurt of his person and the disgrace of his authority I do hereby publicly confess myself guilty of a most notorious breach of the peace and do heartily and sincerely ask pardon of him and all others whom I may have offended by my said behaviour.

"And it is ordered that the same be entered to remain a record as a precedent punishment for the like offender if it be thought sufficient or requisite."

One other scene. Few who saw it will forget the coronation year of King Edward VII. Like other towns, Maidenhead was all astir with preparations for the occasion, when the whole nation was staggered by the news of the King's illness and the postponement of the great event. The Corporation was in session in the Town Hall, not only in connection with the festivities, but also to hear the Mayor announce that Alderman Nicholson had offered to present the town with a site for the library, which Mr. Carnegie had given a few days previously, and a large number of burgesses were also present. Rumours respecting the King had been current all the afternoon, and when these were now confirmed blank dismay prevailed and no one knew what to do. A few necessary arrangements were made, and then a Councillor rose and suggested an immediate adjournment to St. Mary's Church, with a request to the Chaplain to lead them in prayer to Almighty God that the threatened national disaster might be averted. The suggestion, which in some circumstances might have been received coldly, seemed now to voice the universal feeling, for there are moments in the history of a community as in the life of an individual, when the soul instinctively seeks communion with the unseen. Instantly every man in the hall rose and formed up in a procession, which, led by the Mayor, Councillor Good, in a few moments was solemnly and silently pacing through the street to the House of God. The scene was possibly all the more impressive from its spontaneity, and the fact that, with the exception of the Mayor, who had just had time to put on his badge, nearly every man present was in a straw hat and summer attire. The Church was packed to the door. Rarely has Isaac Watts' hymn " O God our help in ages past " been sung with deeper feeling, rarely has the noble language of the Prayer Book seemed more beautifully appropriate; and when the great congregation joined in the National Anthem, sung *pianissimo,* there was hardly a dry eye in the church. This was Tuesday, the 24th of June, 1902.

CHAPTER VI.

THE HIGH STEWARDS.

THE office of High Steward is one about which there must always be some uncertainty, both as to position and duties, not because there are no data, but because procedure and custom varied so considerably in different boroughs and in Webb Eng. Loc. Gov., p. 321. different reigns. As Corporations came to control the various Courts which grew up or were granted by Charter, there was often an official appointed to preside over them who was possessed of legal knowledge, and combined more or less the functions of Steward and Recorder. In process of time the tendency was to separate these offices, and then the Steward, or High Steward, became in some cases a subordinate officer, in some others he continued one of the chiefs of the Corporation, and sometimes the office became a sinecure and the duties were performed by deputy. But in a very large proportion of cases the High Steward became "an officer of great dignity, and some influence, but with practically no duties or emoluments; usually a gentleman of high position, and required indeed by the charters of many towns to be an 'eminent,' an 'illustrious,' or a 'distinguished' man." The chief object seemed to be to secure an influential protector at Court. Such was, in the main, the High Steward of

Maidenhead, though up to 1835 he attended meetings of the Council, sat as one of the Borough Justices, and took a more or less prominent part in the public government of the town. The Act of 1835, though it made no provision for the continuance of the office so far as Maidenhead was concerned, did not abolish it, and the Corporation have continued to elect High Stewards, though the office is now purely honorary.

As with the Chaplains, so with the High Stewards, it is not possible to present a complete list. Authority for electing individuals to this office was conferred on the town by the Charter of James II., 1685, but there had been High Stewards elected long before. There was such an election in 1611, though the name of the person elected is not known. Amongst those who have held the office are the following :—

	?	1611	
Sir Richard Lovelace (circ)	1623		
Daniel Blagrave, M.P.	1651	27	Oct.
Sir Edmund Sawyer (circ)	1660		
Sir Robert Sawyer	1678	7	Jan.
James Paine	1692	30	Dec.
Sir Humphrey Foster	1696	8	Sept.
Rt. Hon. Henry St. John (Lord Bolingbroke)	1712	1	Feb.
Sir John Werden, Bt.			
Richard Powney	1758	23	Feb.
Penystone Portlock Powney	1764	25	Oct.
George Vansittart	1794	4	June
[John Sawyer—declined]	1825	30	March
Charles Sawyer	1825	12	April

Side-notes (left margin):

Municip. Corp. Rep.

Municip. Corp. Rep.
Heralds' Visitation, 1623.
R. 189, p. 35a.
R. 189, p. 267.
R. 189, p. 63.
I. 65, p. 123.
R. 189, p. 76.
R. 190, p. 135.
R. 190, p. 135.
R. 190, p. 148.
R. 190, p. 286.
R. 190.
R. 190.

William Henry Grenfell   1884   4 April
    (Lord Desborough)

DANIEL BLAGRAVE came of a prominent
and distinguished Reading family, his uncle
being a mathematician of some eminence. He
himself was born in 1603, and became M.P. for
Reading in 1648, for which town he was also
Recorder from 1645 till his dismissal in 1656.
He was, however, re-instated in 1658. He was
a strong Parliamentarian, and his signature
appears on the death warrant of Charles I. He
was also an Exegenter of the Court of Common
Pleas, a Master in Chancery, Parliamentary
Treasurer for Berks, and one of the Commissioners for the ejection of scandalous and
inefficient ministers. At the Restoration he fled
the Kingdom, and died at Aachen in 1668, in
his 66th year.

The minute of the Corporation appointing Maid. R. 189,
p. 35a.
Mr. Blagrave High Steward is both long and
quaint, and concludes by desiring Mr. Whitfield
" to attend the said Mr. Blagrave and give him
Thanks for his former love to this Corporation
and acquaint him with the said election and
nomination, and to intreate him on the Warden
and Corporation's behalfe to accept the same,
and to owne and assist the said Corporation in
all there lawful applications to the Parliament
or any other Court or Authority."

SIR EDMUND SAWYER came of a Norfolk
family. Born in 1579, he purchased the manor
of Heywood, Berks, in 1627, and settled there.
He died 16th June, 1670. His first wife, a
daughter of Alderman Robert Bathurst of

London, survived her wedding day only three weeks. His second wife was the daughter of Sir William Whitmore of London.

Dict. Nat. Biog.

Sir Edmund bore his part in public affairs, yet still living the life of a country gentleman. He was Auditor of the City of London. His

Cal. St. Pap. Dom.

name appears on a certificate (13th October, 1634) of arrears of stipend due to the Rev. John Dawson, the litigious Chaplain of St. Mary's. It is evident he was also a strong "King's man."

Cal. St. Pap. Dom.

Under date 18th July, 1640, he writes from Heywood to Secretary Windebank about affairs at Maidenhead. Twenty-two of Cap. Edward Andrews' men have run away. Thomas Goldsmith of Maidenhead, and John Winch and John Peverel of Bray, committed for refusing press-money, have escaped. Sir Edmund thinks that " if they were sent for and committed until they conform it would somewhat alter the opinion of the Country touching His Majesty's power of pressing."

SIR ROBERT SAWYER, the fourth son of the foregoing, was born at Heywood in 1633, and

Dic. Nat. Biog.

educated at Cambridge, being chamber-fellow there with Samuel Pepys. His memory is cherished as a benefactor of the library of

Macaulay's History.

Magdalen College. Devoting himself to the law, he became Treasurer of the Inner Temple, and a member of the Oxford Circuit. Wycombe returned him to Parliament in 1673, and four years later he was knighted. Ill-health prevented his holding the office of Speaker of the House of Commons for more than one month. On 14th February, 1681, he became Attorney-

General, and an argument of his against the City of London in a case of Quo Warranto is spoken of as a "masterpiece" of forensic skill. He appeared in the prosecutions relating to the Rye House Plot and Titus Oates, and in both these, as in many other cases, he served the King well—perhaps too well. There were, however, lengths to which he refused to go, and when James sought to exercise dispensing powers and to grant certain patents of exemption merely on his own kingly authority, Sir Robert had to ask His Majesty to find some more complaisant tool to carry out his wishes. This led to his retention as counsel for the Seven Bishops in the historic trial of 1688. His great ability came out conspicuously on that occasion, but could not obscure the fact of his previous harshness in the royal cause. Elected to Parliament for Cambridge University in 1689, his enemies were too strong for him, and he was expelled the House. Their triumphing was, however, short, and one month later he again appeared as the chosen of Cambridge, Sir Isaac Newton recording his vote for him, as he considered that even if he had been over-zealous, he had been sufficiently punished. He died at Highclere, 30th July, 1692. Roger North says he was "a proper comely gentleman inclining to the red; a good general scholar, and perhaps too much of that, in shew at least, which made some account him inclined to be pedantic." Burnet says he was "a dull, hot, man, and forward to serve all the designs of the Court."

HENRY ST. JOHN, afterwards LORD Dic. Nat. Biog.

BOLINGBROKE, who was also High Steward
of Newbury, has been justly described as " one
of the very ablest men who ever filled a conspicuous place in the Councils of the British
State." He was born in 1678, lost his mother
at an early age, and came under the care of a
grandmother, whose ideas of education consisted
mainly in giving large doses of the Commentaries
of that Dr. Manton, whose pride it was to have
produced one hundred and nineteen sermons on
the one hundred and nineteenth Psalm. Eton
and Oxford were more to the lad's taste, and he
left Christ Church well read in the classics, both
of the ancients, and of his own nation. Parliament received him when barely twenty-three
years old, as the representative of Wootton
Bassett, and in 1700 he married Miss Winch-
combe, a descendant of the celebrated Jack of
Newbury. The union was not a happy one;
money had been its attraction, and St. John's
conduct resulted in a separation. At the time
of his election to the High Stewardship of
Maidenhead in 1711-2, St. John was Secretary
of State for War, and gradually practically the
entire control of the foreign policy of the nation
came into his hands. He was created Viscount
Bolingbroke in 1712, but in spite of this advance-
ment dark days were hastening on. Differences
with his colleagues resulted in the triumph
of Bolingbroke for one short week, at the end
of which the Queen died, George I. ascended
the throne, and Bolingbroke, who had been
intriguing with the Stuarts, was attainted of
treason and fled to France. Loyal to the House

of Brunswick, the men of Maidenhead hasted to purge themselves of all complicity with the evil deeds of their High Steward, and on 3rd March, 1715-6, they solemnly and formally discharged R. 189. p. 55. him from his office.

Later on Bolingbroke was allowed to return to England, when, settling at Dawley, near Uxbridge, the once brilliant statesman quietly occupied himself with farming and literature.

RICHARD POWNEY, of All Souls, Oxford, served the borough with which his family was most intimately connected for many years both as Recorder and High Steward. Perhaps his chief distinction is that he was the Editor of the Earl of Clarendon's "State Letters and Diary," which were printed in 1763. Mr. Powney died June 23rd, 1764.

PENYSTONE PORTLOCK POWNEY, the nephew of the foregoing, was the son of Penystone Powney, M.P. for Berks, who on the death of a maternal relative had inherited the Ives Place estate, through whom the same passed to his son, who made it his residence. In 1786, Penystone Portlock Powney, whose mother was a Miss Portlock of Bedford, purchased Ockwells Manor, being at that time M.P. for Windsor, and having succeeded to his father's office of Verderer, or Superintendent of trees in the royal forest. His death occurred on 17th January, 1794, at the age of fifty-two.

GEORGE VANSITTART, sixth son of Arthur Vansittart, of Shottesbrook, was born 15th September, 1745. His earlier life was spent in India in the service of the East India

Company, being employed partly in administration and partly in commerce. He is said to have been a good man of business and an accomplished linguist. He became a member of the Supreme Council of Bengal and was a friend and supporter of Warren Hastings. Returning to England, he purchased the Bisham Abbey estate in 1780, and for twenty-eight years represented Berkshire in Parliament. He died 24th January, 1825, and an entry in the Corporation Minutes testifies to the great respect in which he was held locally. It was ordered that the Chapel be hung with black, and the bell be tolled. Nor was his popularity undeserved, for to his other excellencies he added a kind heart, refusing to raise the rents of any of his farms though war was being waged, and landowners were raising rents all round, believing as he did that such practices were oppressive, if not indeed unjust, to the farmers. His memory is perpetuated by a mural tablet in St. Mary's Church.

Maid.
R. 190.

CHARLES SAWYER, who was the third member of his family sustaining the office of High Steward, was born at Heywood, Berks, on 23rd January, 1787, and was educated at Eton and Christ Church, Oxford. Entering the Army, he served with the 16th Light Dragoons under Wellington in the Peninsular War. He was invalided home, and married, in 1812, Henrietta, daughter of Admiral Sir George Bowyer, Bart. He resided at Altwood, Maidenhead, till his father's death, when he moved to Heywood, where he died in 1876, at the ripe age of 89. He was a magistrate and Deputy-

Lieutenant for Berks, Vice-Chairman of Quarter Sessions, and an active Poor Law Guardian of the Cookham Union. Of his sons, Major Edmund Sawyer was one of the first officers of the Maidenhead Volunteer Rifle Corps; Mr. Robert Sawyer became Recorder of Maidenhead, and the Reverend William G. Sawyer was for many years the respected vicar of St. Luke's, Maidenhead.

On the passing of the Municipal Corporation Act of 1835 no provision was made for continuing the office of High Steward. On the other hand, the Act did not abolish it, and the new Corporation saw no reason why that office should not be continued, although the holder would have no formal duties, and no voting power in the reformed Council. Mr. Sawyer was accordingly approached on 4th June, 1836, and requested " to resume the function of an office he so honourably and usefully exercised under the old Corporation." Mr. Sawyer consented by a letter dated three days later. On his death in 1876, no steps were taken to fill the office till a Committee on the Charters and Muniments of the Borough reported in 1884 in favour of filling the vacancy.

WILLIAM HENRY GRENFELL, raised to the peerage as LORD DESBOROUGH of Taplow, in 1905, and made a Knight of the Garter in 1928, accepted the High Stewardship in 1884. Born in 1855, educated at Harrow and Baliol College, Oxford, Lord Desborough has won distinction in many fields, though perhaps his conspicuous success in all forms of athletics has somewhat obscured the fact that these are not his only achievements. He has been President of the Oxford University Athletic and Boating Clubs, has swum across Niagara, stroked an eight across the English Channel, done some remarkable mountaineering, won punting and other championships and prizes almost without number, and taken a leading part in the organisation of the great International "Olympic" gatherings of recent years. But in addition to all this, Lord Desborough has found time for literary, as well as parliamentary, municipal, and other public pursuits. He has served as a War Correspondent, as Chairman of the Thames Conservancy, as Chairman of the Chambers of Commerce first of London, and then of the Empire, and both in 1895 and 1896 as Mayor of Maidenhead.

TOWN HALL—1847.

The Corner Shop and Post Office occupy the site of the old Bear Hotel.

CHAPTER VII.

THE TOWN HALL.

HE Town Hall, or, as it was originally called, the Guildhall, has always occupied its present position at the Market Place. When it was first erected is not known, but it is fair to suppose that after the founding of the Maidenhead Guild in 1451 that body cast about for a residence, and there is no reason to doubt but what they either established themselves in one of the rooms of the Market House, or built something there for their accommodation. The building was probably not a large one, but either then or later it contained rooms allotted to the Town Serjeant. Land at the rear belonging to the Corporation was later on occupied by tenements, one of which was let in the reign of James I. to Thomas Aldridge, a shoemaker, for 4s. per annum, and Maid. J. 81. in 1791 there was also standing there a structure Maid. J. 105. called the "Dutch Barn."

To the North of the Market House, and separated from it by a road some 6 ft. wide, Maid. K. 137. stood an ancient tenement called Copped Hall. "Copped" means peaked, or crested, and probably indicates a structure with a high pitched gable roof. The land on which Copped Hall stood was that granted by Queen Margaret, widow of Edward I., to Adam le Spicer, 26th April, 1313, the same land which was erroneously supposed to have been given for the founding of St. Mary's Chapel, although it is some distance from the site of the Chapel, and St. Mary's had been built forty years before the date of this grant, and the land measured only thirty feet by twelve feet—surely rather small for a chapel. The exact date of the erection of Copped Hall is not known, but the structure is described in a deed of Henry VI. (1431) as "two shops with solars above built." It is curious to note that whoever drew up the "Abstract of Title" of this property has connected "above built" with "shops" instead of with "solars," supposing that "solars" meant "cellars." As a matter of fact a "solar" was a large room, lofty, and in the upper part of the house, and was usually set at the disposal of visitors.

Copped Hall passed through many hands. At one time (1431) its owner rejoiced in the name of Bar-vote Horn, which the learned have translated Barefoot Horn. Its latest proprietor was Joseph Trone, who sold it to the Corporation 14th June, 1751, for £90. It was at once pulled down; its beams went to help build the new parsonage for St. Mary's, and its site was added to that of the old Town Hall, which was also pulled down, together with the Sergeant's House and all other connected buildings, to make way for a new Hall, erected in 1777, which cost £1,330. The old material was sold to the Recorder, Mr. James Payn, for £100.

The Contractors were Mr. Thomas Emblin and Mr. John Cooper. Thomas Emblin is believed to be a relation of Henry Emblin (or

Marginal notes:

Maid. K. 120.

Maid. K. 118.

Horne's Manor & Manorial Records.

Maid. K. 120.

Maid. R. 189, p. 78.

Maid. R. 190.

Emlyn as he is usually called) who carried out
extensive works of reparation at St. George's
Chapel, Windsor, in 1788, and who designed
and executed the cement organ screen therein,
which has been cited as one of the best works
of its time. His sister married the above Mr.
John Cooper, who personally executed the carpenter's work in the royal pew. The designs for
Maidenhead Town Hall, prepared by Mr. Keen
and carried out by Messrs. Emblin and Cooper,
together with the original contract, are preserved
in the Borough Museum. The elevation, however, does not correspond with what undoubtedly
occupied the site a century later, but whether
the design was modified, or there was a subsequent alteration, there is no evidence to show.

In the North East corner, and facing High
Street, a leaden tablet was affixed to the stone-
work bearing the following inscription :— R. 190, p. 202.

THE FOUNDATION STONE

OF

THIS EDIFICE

was laid on the 13th day of June in the year of our
Lord, 1777,

in the 17th year of the Reign of his Majesty,
George the 3rd,

By ABRAHAM DARBY, Esq., Mayor,

In the presence of the Corporation of Maidenhead:

Penyston Powney, Esq., High Steward.
Robert Vansittart, Esq., Recorder
Richard Taylor ⎫
Aspin Taylor ⎭ Bridgemasters.

John Gould
William Rose
John Clark
John Boult
John Butterfield } Burgesses.
John Laughton
James Atlee
Henry Emblin

James Payn, Town Clerk.

Theodosius Keene,
Surveyor.

Thomas Emblin,
John Cooper,
Builders.

In those days there was a door-way in the East side of the building, which led to a covered way passing over Park Street, and giving a communication with the Bear Hotel, which then stood at the corner of Park Street and High Street. Underneath the Hall, and to the rear of the Market Place, were the licensed premises of the Fighting Cocks Inn. In 1794, on June 18th, a furious storm broke over Maidenhead. The hail was terrific, and the Town Hall felt its full force. £19 10s. 0d. was the bill for repairing and glazing its broken windows. The Hall was again altered in 1878, when the seating capacity of the main room was more than doubled, and the licensed premises below were removed.

Maid. I. 66.
p. 32.

Three tablets are affixed to its walls and approaches. One of a funereal character on the staircase bears the names of those who formed the Corporation at the re-building in 1878. The north wall of the Hall itself bears a painting of the royal arms of the time of Charles II., and is dated 1660. It is surrounded by a pedimented frame on which is carved a representation of the borough seal, though the inscription has not been copied quite correctly. It runs Sg IOHIS, CODA-BGAN, THIERN. It is thought that this is the coat of arms which was once displayed in St. Mary's, and that it was removed to the Hall on the re-building of the Church. All churches were required to set up the royal arms at the time of the Restoration.

The third tablet is on the West wall, is of brass, in a carved oak frame, and bears a tribute to the Maidenhead men who took part in the Boer War. The following is the inscription :—

1899 SOUTH AFRICA 1902

The undermentioned Officers and Men being inhabitants of Maidenhead volunteered for Active Service with the Imperial Forces in South Africa during the Boer War, 1899-1902.

IMPERIAL YEOMANRY: Lieut. A. C. Pallant, T. Haig. Lieut. & Qmr. N. P. Snowden, J. Blockley. Q.M. Sergt. K. S. Gardner. Far. Sergt. A. E. Neeve, D. Beeson, F. E. Rackstraw, Sergt. F. W. Harmer, E. Sable. Corpl. A. Lynn (died of disease), F. S. Bampton, G. F. Bailey, G. Bond, C. Russell, C. Durrant. Lance Corp. A. E. Aldridge, Priv. G. B. Darby, F. H. Russell, F. Humfrey, A. J. Gilroy, A. G. Groves (died of disease), W. R. Nicholson, W. Sexton, A. Smith, W. Colliass, H. F. Humphreys, J. Saunders, T. E. Bowman, B. E. Meade, H. S. Webber.

CORPS OF ELECTRICAL ENGINEERS: Capt. J. E. Pearce. I. V. B. ROYAL BERKS REGT.: Lieut. W. P. Alleyne. Corp. A. J. Taylor. Lce. Corp. H. Littleton, E. J. Wood, T. Maguire. Priv. T. Allam, H. W. Blackwell, A. Campey, R. Groves (died of disease), C. Harris, C. Lee (killed in action), E. R. Littleton, C. Maynard, F. W.

Moore, W. Platford, W. H. Roles, W. Crosby, H. Simmonds, F. West, A. Goom.

COMPOSITE CYCLE CORPS: Priv. H. H. Moore, T. R. Nash.

CHAPTER VIII.

THE REGALIA.

THE SEAL. Maidenhead has never received a grant of arms, and strictly speaking there are no Borough Arms.

It possesses, however, and has for many years used, a seal, in the centre of which is a head—full-face—with long hair, bearing round it the inscription S Johis Godayn Can Thiern, a contraction for Sigillum Johannis Godayn Canonici Thiernensis, which is, being interpreted, The seal of John Godayn, Canon of Thiers. Who John Godayn was, or how his private seal passed to and became the official seal of the Corporation, are problems that have vexed many minds, and are still as far from solution as ever. All we can say is that in Auvergne in France, at a place called Thiers, or more anciently Thiern, there was a collegiate church with twelve Canons, and, as the name Godayn is certainly French, it seems reasonable to suppose John Godayn to have been one of them. Beyond that it is unfortunately impossible to go. The seal is mounted with an ivory handle, but a small ring fixed to the end of the brass seal itself suggests that its former owner probably wore it about his person, possibly suspended by a cord round his neck. The earliest document in the possession of the Corporation to which the seal is attached bears date 12th February, 1612.

THE MACES. Of these there are two, one large and the other much smaller, but both handsome works of art, silver gilt. The smaller is the more ancient, and may possibly date from the Charter of James I. (1604), when two Sergeants at Mace were appointed to attend on the Warden and carry silver or gilt maces before him. The only record on the subject in the Corporation Minutes is an entry on 9th April, 1683, when it was ordered that "the Mace of the Corporation be enlarged and made more graceful." One, Mr. George Gray, was to be asked "for his assistance in managing the alteration of the said mace for the better accommodation," and £10 was allowed for the expense of the same. After the purchase of the large Mace the smaller and older one was allowed to get sadly out of repair. Broken and battered, its miserable condition spoke eloquently of that want of reverence for the past, that lack of appreciation of the value of historic continuity, which has sometimes characterised our Nation. Fortunately there were those who were not given over absolutely to utilitarianism, but who could recognise a work of art, and a valuable link with bygone times. Mr. William Morris took the old mace in hand in 1885, and in commemoration of his Recordership had it thoroughly repaired and restored. It is now carefully preserved as one of the choicest treasures of the Corporation.

The large Mace, silver gilt, dates from 1776, at least that is the date inscribed upon it. The bowl may be unscrewed from the shaft below,

Maid. R. 189. p. 275.

THE MACES AND THE MAYOR'S CHAIN.

and the crown covering above, and then forms a handsome drinking vessel. Many a Mayor has toasted and been toasted therewith, and often has it gone round as a " loving cup." It has had in its time more stirring adventures still. Several times it has gone round the Borough " beating the bounds," passing through windows, over hedges, and down mid-stream. Once, in a box at that time somewhat dilapidated, it arrived at the door of a newly-elected and highly nervous Mayor. " What is that thing? " exclaimed his worship. The servant did not know; it was a box brought by some man who said he was to leave it there. " Take it out of the house at once! " cried the newly-elected, for it was the time of Fenian troubles, and who could say but what it was an " infernal machine " devised for the special destruction of Maidenhead's chief citizen! Taken out it was, and in the woodhouse it reposed, till someone plucked up courage to look inside the awe-inspiring box, and discovered the glittering symbol of authority.

THE CHAIN dates from 1880, and was obtained largely through the efforts of Councillor Richard Illsley, who resolved to signalise his third successive year of Mayoralty by acquiring for the Corporation this particular badge of office, which, as public functions multiplied, had become a practical necessity. Each link is of gold, is in the shape of a shield, and is surmounted by a mural crown. It bears on the obverse the crest or motto of the Mayor, whose name and year of office are inscribed on the reverse. The links are connected by small circular rose pattern links, and to the centre one is attached the large jewelled badge or pendant, bearing the Borough Arms in proper colours. This badge cost £65, the money being collected by Councillor (now Alderman) C. W. Cox, then the junior member of the Corporation.

Maid. R. 190.

THE ROBES. By an entry in the Council Minutes dated 30th March, 1705, it was "ordered that every member of the Corporation provide himself with a decent gown, such as are generally used by members of Corporations," and later,

Maid. R. 189, p. 69.

on 28th May, 1729, that the Mayor and Burgesses " shall have gowns of black cloth, and appear in the Chapel of the said Corporation on Whitsunday next after the date hereof under the penalty of forfeiting each person so offending or neglecting the sum of five pounds." In the course of years the custom of robing fell into disuse, and the robes themselves into disrepair. The whole of them were sold as useless lumber in 1862 by the then Mayor, who also parted with the halberds, staves, stocks and all he could lay his hands on, such things being in his opinion "the relics of a barbarous age." The Mayor did not again appear in official garb till 1870, when Mr. Robert Walker, the father of the present writer, signalised his year of office by purchasing at his own cost a Mayor's Robe, and presenting it to the town. Robes for the entire Corporation were re-introduced in 1910, and were first used at a Memorial Service for King Edward VII. on May 22 of that year.

THE BRIDGEMASTERS' STAVES. Of these there are four, two longer and two shorter,

and it is possible they were allocated to the
Senior and Junior Bridgemaster respectively.
Each has a brass cap inscribed

John Cowley, Warden
Bridgemaster
Thomas Russell
Richard Baker,

together with a crowned head, and the date
1667. In the woodwork are painted the royal
arms surmounted by W R IIII and beneath is
the date 1827. Of course in 1827 the monarch
was George IV., and not William, and a close
inspection reveals the fact that the W is painted
over some other letter or mark. Doubtless the
staves were painted in the reign of George IV.,
and when William became King " W " was
substituted for " G " without altering the date.

THE HALBERDS. There are two of these,
one a little longer than the other, but otherwise
they are almost identical in pattern. Where they
came from or when they were acquired is not
known. The longer is inscribed "Coldstream $\frac{11}{3}$,"
and the shorter with certain marks which look
like SA OP M [? Salop M].

THE PIKES. Of these also there are two.
They bear no inscriptions, but with the halberds
and Bridgemasters' Staves they have been
carried in municipal processions for many years
past. These pikes, together with the halberds
and staves, were purchased at the sale above
referred to by Mr. Rutland of Taplow, who later
on generously gave them back to the Corporation, who are not likely to let them go from their
hands again.

CHAPTER IX.

THE COURTS AND THE RECORDERS.

BY the Charter of Elizabeth (1581-2) authority was given for holding certain courts, and the first of these was a Court of Record. It was to be held every three weeks, on a Monday, before the Warden and Bridgemasters or two of them, and to deal with all manner of trespasses, offences, contracts, debts, &c., concerning Maidenhead Bridge or its support, with all powers of attachments, distresses, caption of bodies, and so forth. The Charter of James I. altered the day to Wednesday, and extended the jurisdiction of the Court to all pleas personal and mixed, provided both parties were residents, and the cause of action did not exceed £20. The Charter of James II. simply altered the day to Friday.

A Court of Record is defined by Stephen in his Commentary on the Laws of England as one " whereof the acts and judicial proceedings are enrolled for a perpetual memorial and testimony; which rolls are called the records of the Court." He adds, " no other court hath authority to fine and imprison for contempt of its authority. So that the very erection of a new jurisdiction with the power of fine or imprisonment for contempt makes it a court of record."

Maid. R. 198. The Memorials preserved with the Corporation muniments include a large volume containing the minutes of a Court of Record from 9th

January, 1740, to 12th June, 1835, and a _{Maid. E. 32-36} number of parchments containing chiefly oaths of allegiance and declarations against that " impious and heretical and damnable doctrine and position that Princes excommunicated or deprived by the Pope or any authority of the See of Rome may be deposed or murdered by their subjects or any other whatsoever." There are also several minutes and records of a Court of Quarter Sessions, which was also a Court of Record, and is sometimes difficult to distinguish _{Maid. E. 193.} from the Court above named. The earliest of these minutes now in the possession of the Corporation dates from September, 1690, to the end of 1740. Latin is the language used up to 30th March, 1733, the first entry in English bearing date 13th April of that year.

At the beginning of the 19th century the Court of Record seems to have lapsed, but on 25th September, 1822, the Corporation passed a resolution to re-establish it and resume it on Friday, 18th October, 1822, "for the recovery of debts not exceeding £20." A table of fees was drawn up and is recorded with the above entry.

From very early times it was customary to _{Municip. Corp. Rep.} elect a Recorder, but on the passing of the Municipal Corporations Act, 1835, both Recorder and Quarter Sessions ceased to be, while the Court of Record had again lapsed. All three might, however, have been resuscitated if the Corporation had thought well to take the necessary steps, and for a time they contemplated so doing. A Committee was appointed early in January, 1836, to obtain from the King in Council the grant of a Court of Quarter Sessions, and £40 was named as the salary proposed to be given to the Recorder who would be appointed to preside in such Court. The Town Clerk also was instructed to take the necessary steps to re-establish the Court of Record. Nothing effectual, however, was done, and in September, 1836, all matters relating to the Quarter Sessions and Recorder were adjourned *sine die,* and the Town Clerk proceeded no further with the Court of Record.

In 1884 a Committee of the Council reported on the Borough Charters and Minutes, and drew attention to the ancient custom of appointing a Recorder, and shortly after, 2nd May, 1884, Mr. William Morris was offered, and he accepted, the office. He died on 14th December, 1886, and on the 7th January following, Mr. Robert Sawyer, a member of the family which had given more than one High Steward to the town, was elected Recorder. He resigned the position some years later on the ground that he had no court, no jurisdiction and no emoluments. It is to be feared the appointments of both Mr. Morris and Mr. Sawyer were irregular, as such appointments can only be made by the Crown.

Of the past Recorders of Maidenhead practically nothing is known, but it may safely be said that few, if any, were more intimately connected with town matters, or exercised a greater influence in the community than Mr. James Payn, who was Recorder from 17th October, 1800, till his death on 22nd January, 1822. From 1779 he was also County Treasurer for Berks. It is said he came

News of a
Country
Town
(Townsend).

to Maidenhead poor. He was anything but poor
at his death, and his removal was felt to be a
genuine loss to the community. A tablet in
St. Mary's Church perpetuates his memory, and
his portrait, presented to the Corporation by his
daughter, still hangs in one of the rooms of the Maid. R. 190.
Town Hall.

The Charter of Elizabeth granted yet another
Court, viz., the Court of Pie Powder. This
singular title is a corruption of the old French
pied puldreux, and the institution itself was a
common accompaniment of fairs and markets. It
was a " court of summary jurisdiction as to Hone's
"Manor
contracts for goods bought or sold, for battery & Manorial
Records."
or disturbance, or for words as to slander of
wares in the Market there." It took cognizance
of all offences committed in a market or fair.
The Mayor was the presiding judge, and offence, Blackstone's
Com.
complaint, judgment, and execution of sentence
all took place so speedily that some have
attempted to connect this celerity with the name—
it was as quick as the shaking the dust from
your foot. Others have traced the name to the
dusty feet of the suitors, while some affirm that
" dusty foot " was a recognised name for a Pettingall
Maid. Pub.
pedlar, as it certainly was for a countryman, Library.
from his dirty or dusty shoes, the result of rural
employments, and this not only in old French
but among the Greeks also. Courts similar to
Pye Powder were known to the Romans, were in
use in England amongst the Normans, and a Palgrave on
Courts of Pye
statute of Edward III. declares such a court to Powder.
Maid. Pub.
be " of right pertaining " to all fairs. They Library.
have long since become obsolete.

The Charter of Elizabeth also granted the right to hold a Court taking over-sight of the weights and measures of the town. It was called "The Clerk of the Markets' Court," and was presided over by the Mayor. A jury was sworn, and six other persons were sworn as "tryers," their duty being to keep a record of the persons using scales, weights or measures, to inspect the same, and to report inaccuracies to the Court.

Three foolscap minute-books of its proceedings are preserved in the Municipal Archives, calendared respectively as R199, R200, and R201, and covering the periods from 2nd October, 1761, to 17th October, 1800; 16th January, 1801, to 22nd October, 1819; and 14th January, 1820, to 4th July, 1834, after which there is no record.

The Jury varied in numbers from 12 to 19, but the usual number was 13, and once, on 16th January, 1801, mention is made of a Grand Jury as well.

At first, the Court seems to have been constituted and the "tryers" appointed in the autumn of each year, but subsequently this was done in January, and the Court met by adjournment three or four times in the twelve months, non-attendance after having been duly summoned being visited with a 6s. 8d. fine.

The first record shows that in the first year of George III. there were 80 traders in Maidenhead using scales, weights, and measures. Of these, 40 resided on the Bray side and 40 on the Cookham side of the town. No record is preserved of the occupations of those on the

Cookham side, but the 40 on the Bray side included ten publicans, one cider-maker, one maltster, two bakers, one tallow-chandler, two collar-makers, three butchers, one sack-weaver, one fellmonger, one tripe-woman, one draper, six farmers and gardeners, one meal-man, two blacksmiths, one coal merchant, one tanner, and three general shop-keepers.

Everyone paid a fee of 4d., but there is no statement as to why, or what became of the money.

The fines inflicted varied from 6s. 8d. to 30s., and were not infrequently accompanied by an order for the destruction of the defective weight, measure or scales.

In October, 1812, the " tryers " seem to have made a raid on the inn-keepers, and the landlords of " The Fox and Horn," " The Hand and Flowers," " The Bull," " The Red Lion," and " The Quart Pot " all came to grief under penalties of 10s. and 2s. 6d. costs. So did another landlord, whose quart cups were deficient by half a pint and his pint measure by a quarter of a pint. This gentleman kept a house bearing the appropriate name of " The Fleece."

Towards the end of its existence, the Court did very little business, the usual memorandum being : " The jury returned that they had not any presentments to make to this Court." But, whatever they did or did not, they appear to have required a fair amount of " creature comfort "—so much so that, under date of 1st October, 1796, it was resolved by the Town Council, " that the jury and ' tryers ' having run the Corporation to a great expense for refreshments contrary to express order, it is ordered that no dinner, liquor or other allowance be made them in future."

Maid. R. 190.

Maid. I. 65, p. 54.

It is interesting to note that it is in connexion with the refreshments of this Court that the first mention is made of tobacco. " 16 July, 1675, Paid per Mr. Warden's order for wine, beer, and tobacco upon the King's Clerk of the Markets, 6s. 2d."

This account may be fitly closed by quoting the remarkable presentment handed in by the foreman of the jury on the 11th April, 1834, the last sitting but one of the Court :—" The Worshipful the Mayor and Corporation of the town of Maidenhead. Gentlemen,—In presenting you with the result of the inspection of your Trials Jury, which took place on Thursday, the 3rd of this month, they, as a matter of course (rather than of justice), have nothing to present before you.—I remain, Gentlemen, yours most respectfully, James Coster, foreman of this useless jury (as at present constituted)."

The legislature appears to have appraised the Court at a similar value, for a record in the minutes of the Maidenhead Court of Quarter Sessions, under date 17th October, 1834, states that, by virtue of a recent Act of Parliament, James Fuller was that day appointed Inspector of Weights and Measures, and thereafter we hear no more of the Court of the Clerk of the Market.

Maid. R. 197.

On the establishment of County Councils in 1888, the original standards were removed to Reading, but were returned and formally handed over to the Corporation on 28th September, 1927, and placed in the Public Museum.

Doubtless the business of all these courts was well executed, and justice administered with due dignity. The records do not indicate that the magistrates were over - worked, and lighter incidents occasionally relieved the tedium of the proceedings. There were certain officials in Georgian days known as Tithingmen and Con- Maid. N. stables, and it fell to the bench to receive and consider their periodical reports. An interesting bundle of these documents is preserved, and testifies that human nature was pretty much then as now, owners showing the same indisposition to repair gates and paths as in more recent times, and people being as ready to encumber streets and ways as to-day. But on the whole Maidenhead could not have been a very bad place, for in the entire six years ending 1835 there were only 17 Municip. Corp. Rep. prisoners tried at the Maidenhead Quarter Sessions.

It was not long before this (about 1828 or Silver. 1829) that an amusing incident occurred. The day was hot, and the worthy Mayor began to feel the job was a dry one, and accordingly sent out the constable for some beer. Having refreshed himself, he courteously invited the Bench to join him, " and," said he, " perhaps the constable would like a little too." That worthy " didn't mind if he did." " Perhaps the prisoner would like a drop as well," said the Mayor, and the prisoner had a turn. Then they proceeded to business, found the prisoner guilty, and sent him down to Reading Gaol.

CHAPTER X.

MAIDENHEAD IN NATIONAL HISTORY.

WHILE it cannot be claimed that Maidenhead has influenced, or even borne very prominent part in the history of England, it has, nevertheless, touched that history in a few points too interesting to be lost.

The first of these is admittedly speculative. But when the Danes under Bagsecg and Halfdene came up the Thames in 870, the "great year of battles," and were defeated at Englefield by Ethelred and Alfred, it is certain they either halted at, or passed by, the old ford where long after was placed the bridge which changed the hamlet of South Ellington into the town of Maidenhead. The late Sir George Young, Bt., has pointed out the practical impossibility of dragging the long Danish ships over the marshes and shallows of Cookham, and argues with considerable force that the Danes must have left their vessels at Maidenhead, and *marched* overland to Reading. This conjecture is strengthened by the fact that the battles were fought over the fords of the Kennet, and not near the Thames.

We are on surer ground when we get to the troubles that arose when Henry IV. seized the throne in 1399, and when Richard II. sought to win it back. The materials for re-constructing this piece of history are furnished by Grafton and other Chroniclers, and particularly by the writings of a French monk of ·St. Denys, who travelled in England about 1380 and subsequently, and who on his return to France published his Latin "Chronicle of the Betrayal and Death of Richard II.," which has been several times translated into French. From these and other writers it appears that "scarcely was Henry warm in his new dignity "—so Grafton puts it—when certain noblemen met at the house of the Abbot of Westminster, whose righteous soul had been much vexed by a declaration of Henry's which no good churchman could be expected to stomach, that, as touching temporalities, "princes had too little and religion too much." They resolved to invite the King to a tournament at Oxford, and then and there to kill him. The plot, however, went awry, chiefly through the cowardice or indecision of the Earl of Rutland, who managed to allow his father, the Duke of York, to learn the secret and warn the King. The whole of this part of the business is powerfully rendered by Shakespeare in "Richard II."

Chronique de la traison et mort de Richart. Deux Roi. d' Engleterre. Williams' translation.

Seeing something had gone wrong, the conspirators made a bold attack on Windsor, but the King had fled to London, rallied the trained bands, and was encamped at Hounslow. The insurgents retired by way of Colnbrook and Maidenhead towards Oxford, but the forces of Henry overtook them on the 7th (or 8th) January, 1400, at Maidenhead Bridge, which the rear-guard of the insurgents so effectually defended that not a man passed over the river for three days, while they managed to capture from King Henry two packhorses, two baggage-waggons, and a chariot. After the third day the Earl of Kent, who had commanded the rearguard, stole off quietly in the dark, taking all the townsfolk with him to serve King Richard. As Kent's party had previously cleared the town of all provisions—which King Henry found out next day to his cost—the good men of Maidenhead thought it was better to feast with the old King than fast with the new. In the long run they had better have stayed at home, for the whole thing came to naught in a few weeks, and the heads of the unfortunate leaders were displayed impaled on London Bridge.

During the Civil War in the time of Charles I. if Maidenhead did not influence national history it certainly felt the effect of what was going on. The bridge is broken down "several times" (11th May, 1654); a Court is held here to adjudicate on certain war prizes (8th November, 1625); a messenger is dispatched to bring up Thomas Davis and John Langton of Maidenhead, defaulters at musters (16th September, 1638); Sir James Harrington writes to the Earl of Northumberland that the first meeting and concentration of regiments into a brigade was on Thursday last at Maidenhead Thicket, "our numbers I then judge to be 3000, from whence that night we marched to Reading" (19th October, 1644); and Cromwell gives orders that Earl Manchester's troop quartered at Maiden-

Cal. St.
Pap. Dom.

Cal. St.
Pap. Dom.

Cal. St.
Pap. Dom.

Cal. St.
Pap. Dom.

Cal. St.
Pap. Dom.

head shall be vigilant in carrying out the desires
of Parliament (20th October, 1644). An entry
in the Corporation Minutes dated 15th May, Maid. R. 189,
1644, is also significant of much. It is there   p. 28a.
ordered that the twenty nobles for the Warden's
dinner shall not be paid for ten years, but shall
go towards the debt of the town.

But for Maidenhead the chief event of all that Clarendon's
time was the memorable and pathetic last inter-   History
view of Charles I. with his children. After the Bk. X., p. 44.
surrender of Oxford these were entrusted to the
Earl of Northumberland, and were at St. James'
Palace or Sion House. Charles, himself a
prisoner at Caversham at the house of Lord
Craven, asked Fairfax if it would be possible
for him to see his little ones. Fairfax laid the
request before Parliament, and even went so far
as to offer his personal guarantee that the
children should be safely returned to London.
" Who, if he can imagine it to be his own case,"
said he, " cannot be sorry if his Majesty's
natural affection to his children in so small a
thing should not be complied with ? " The
interview accordingly took place at Maidenhead
on 16th July, 1647. A well-known picture
locates the scene under a large oak tree near
the east end of St. Mary's Church, and portrays
the King with the little baby Duke of Gloucester
in his arms, the princess Elizabeth leaning on
him and weeping, and the young Duke of York
led by a lady in attendance. Subsequently,
refreshments were taken at the Greyhound Inn
in the High Street (the Westminster Bank now
covers the site) ; but whether we picture the scene

in the open-air or in the old Inn parlour, it is as pathetic a one as need be.

Whatever were the failings and shortcomings of Charles as a king, and they were neither few nor small; as a man his conduct was exemplary, and as a father he was tender and affectionate. As the little ones gathered round his knee it was no wonder his heart was wrung with anguish, for he must by this time have realised that he was not likely to see his children again. It is said that strong men who had faced death on the battle-field unmoved, stood and looked on with tears in their eyes; that Cromwell himself was there that day, and confessed he had never been present at so tender a scene. Later in the day the royal captives drove on to Caversham, and after they had been together for two days the last farewell was said.

The next scene brings us to the days of Charles II. The Civil War is over, the protectorate is ended, the Great Englishman is dead, the restoration is an accomplished fact, and now—for reprisals! The foolish attempt of Charles I. and Laud to impose prelacy on the Scotch was answered, not only by Jenny Geddes' stool, but by a Solemn League and Covenant, whereby those subscribing bound themselves to maintain a presbyterian form of Church government and to resist prelacy. In 1643 the General Assembly of the Scottish Church sent eight Commissioners to treat with the English Parliament for the union of the English and Scottish Churches in one form of ecclesiastical government. The result was the ordinance of

Cambridge
Mod. Hist.
IV. p. 329.

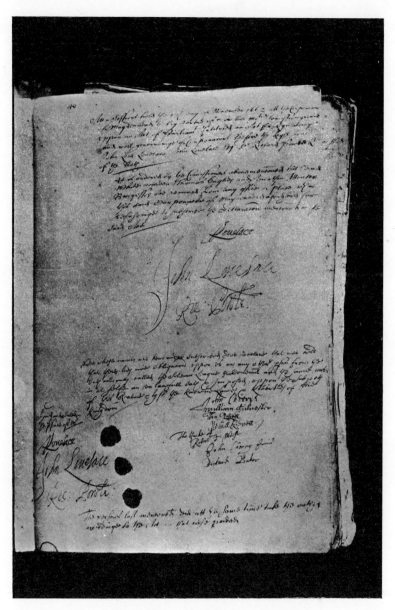

COMMISSION OF ENQUIRY AS TO
THE SOLEMN LEAGUE AND COVENANT.

19th August, 1645, for the election of Elders.
This attempt to establish Presbyterianism was,
however, rendered abortive by the almost simul-
taneous rise to power of the Independents, and Macaulay I. Chap. 2.
Macaulay states that Presbyterianism was
nowhere fully established save in Middlesex and
Lancashire. Berkshire touches neither of these
counties, but the constant traffic from London
to the West brought Maidenhead into closer
relationship with the Metropolis than was enjoyed
by some nearer places, and the authorities doubtless deemed it wise to enquire how far it was
tarred with the "Covenant" brush. Accordingly,
one fine morning, 17th November, 1662, there Maid. R. 189. p. 49.
appeared on the scene three commissioners, the
Right Honourable John, Lord Lovelace; John
Lovelace, Esq.; and Sir Richard Powle, K.C.B.

Lord Lovelace was the second Baron who held
that title, being the son of the nobleman who
built Lady Place on the ruins of the old monastic Dict. Nat. Biog.
house of Our Lady, at Hurley, and John Love-
lace, Esq., was he who succeeded to the title as
third Baron in 1670, distinguished, so says Macaulay's History.
Macaulay, "by his taste, by his magnificence,
and by the audacious and intemperate vehemence
of his Whiggism." At this time he was member of Parliament for Berks, which constituency
he represented from 1661 till his elevation to
the Upper House. He was implicated in the
Rye House Plot of 1683, and later it was in a
subterranean vault beneath the stately apartments of his Berkshire mansion that those
"midnight conferences" were held in support
of the cause of him who was soon to rule

England as William III. More than once Lovelace found himself in the hands of his enemies, but the triumph of his party brought him his recompense, and in 1689 he doubtless found consolation in the Captaincy of the Gentlemen Pensioners, to which position he was then advanced.

D. N. B. Sir Richard Powle was the son of Henry Powle of Shottesbrook. He was M.P. for Berkshire in 1660-1, was Knighted and made K.C.B. in 1661, and died in 1678. His brother Henry was Master of the Rolls, and Speaker of the Convention Parliament.

The Commissioners were armed with all needful powers, and forthwith proceeded to business. The record is in the old Corporation Minute Book, and states that the Commission was " grounded on an Act of Parliament entitled An Act for well governing and regulating of Corporations." That Act demanded, amongst other things, that all who held office must renounce all connexion or complicity with the Solemn League and Covenant. The renunciation stands to this day set forth in that same minute book, signed page after page by burgesses and others, and witnessed by the signatures and seals of the Commissioners. Here it is :—

> " We whose names are hereunder subscribed do declare that we hold that there lies no obligation upon us or any other person from the oath commonly called the Solemn League and Covenant and the same was in itself an unlawful oath and imposed upon the subjects of the Realm

against the known laws and liberties of
the Kingdom."

All, however, do not sign. The Warden's
name is not there, and the names of at least
two of the Corporation are missing. It required
some courage in those days to be loyal to one's
convictions, and such loyalty did not generally
go long unrewarded. It did not here. Behold
the record :—

> " Ordered that Edward White, Warden,
> Thomas Hughes and Jonathan Attwater,
> burgesses, be removed from any office
> or place within the said Corporation of
> Maidenhead aforesaid for refusing to
> subscribe the declaration mentioned in
> the said Act."

Methinks there was matter for conversation
over many a mug of ale that night in Maidenhead.

The Plague, which in this reign wrought such
havoc in London, was felt but slightly in
Maidenhead, yet the town being on a main road,
and with such a considerable stream of traffic
passing through it, it would have been a miracle
if it had wholly escaped. As a matter of fact
it did not. There is preserved in the Treasury
Books under date 9th March, 1666-7, a memorial
from the Excise Commissioners proposing an
allowance of £250 to John Peacock and William
Oaks, late Farmers of Excise of Berks, for
losses at Windsor, Maidenhead, and other
infected towns by the contagion in quarter ended
1665, September 29th. " The contagion was in
several of the great towns on the Western Road,

Brit. Mus.
Cal. Treas.
Bks.

though it was not raging in the said towns, and
continued there but a short time."

But once more the years roll on. It is 1688.
Rumour has it that the Prince of Orange, afterwards to be known as William III., has landed.
They say too that James II. has fled, or is
flying. On which side will Maidenhead range
itself? The problem is not perfectly simple, for
the town is full of Irish soldiers, hired by James
to keep the men of Maidenhead in the path of
virtue. There had also been two battalions of
Scotch Guards—so writes Samuel Pepys, of
diary fame, to Lord Dartmouth on 10th December, 1688—"quartered as I take it at Maidenhead," but "one of them, Lieut. Gen. Douglas,
being himself at their head, could not be prevailed with by him to the contrary, but to a
man, officers and all, before his very face
abandoned him and went away towards the
Prince's forces." Surely it was a wag who
really settled the question, for in the middle of
the night suddenly a company of drummers—or
was it someone with a stick and a tray?—struck
up a Dutch March. Helter-skelter over Maidenhead Bridge went the Irish mercenaries, and
were seen no more. When the forces of William
passed through on their way to London, which
there is good reason to suppose they did, they
were welcomed by a town that had rejected
Stewart duplicity, and acclaimed a Sovereign
whose rule meant constitutionalism and the
supremacy of law.

Brit. Mus.
Bar T. 6 a.

CHAPTER XI.

INNS, COACHES, TRAVELLERS AND VISITORS.

AFTER the men of Maidenhead "had built here a wooden bridge upon piles, it [the town] began to have inns and be so frequented as to outvie its neighbouring mother, Bray, a much more ancient place." So says Camden; but though the bridge was in existence before 1300, the first record in the Bray Court Rolls respecting inns does not occur till 1459, when "Thoman Hille, Tithingman, presented that William Mordall holds an inn called the 'Bulle' and takes exorbitant gain." A similar charge was made in 1489, when it is recorded that "Alice Bukland holds an inn called the Bulle, and takes excessive gain." How many other hosts of the "Bull" had similar charges laid at their door one cannot say, but the tradition was apparently kept up to the nineteenth century, as the landlord was fined for giving short measure so late as October, 1812.

B. C. R.

Kerry 144.

Maid. R. 200.

The "Bull" stood in the High Street, on the south side, at the entrance to Ives Place, and is now known as No. 11 High Street. It would be perhaps going too far to say that the house occupying that site is the original structure, but undoubtedly it is very ancient. It was an inn down to about 1870, at which time Mr. William Wilberforce, brother of the celebrated Bishop of Oxford, took up his residence at Ives Place, discontinued the license of the "Bull" and converted the inn into a chapel and priest-house. It was the same gentleman who prefixed the title of "Saint" to the Ives Place estate, though it has no possible connexion with St. Ives, but takes its name from the Manor of Ive, once in the possession of John Ive, who was summoned for fishing in the Thames with a trammel in 1297. It was confirmed later by Henry VIII. in 1537, to the monastery of Bisham, granted on the dissolution of that house to Ann of Cleves, and still later passed to Richard Whitfield, and then to the Powney family. One cannot but regret the addition of a prefix which obscures the true origin of the name.

The next inn in the order of historic record is the "Bear," though whether it was really of later date is uncertain. Again we turn to the Bray Court Rolls, and again find an uncomplimentary record. The year is 1489. "Presented that John Ffraunces holds an inn called 'the Beyre' and charges an unlawful price for provisions." An entry in the following year indicates that not only was the price excessive, but the company was far from select. The "Bear" stood on what is now 35, High Street, and became one of the most important inns in the town. Its vicinity to the Town Hall gave it an immense advantage, and this was enhanced by a covered way over Park Street giving direct communication between the large room of the Hall and the inn. It ceased to be an inn about 1845.

Prior to this date a number of soldiers were

Margin notes:
Kerry 124.

Kerry 148 (pedigree).

Kerry 144.

B. C. R.

quartered in Maidenhead, at least one troop of Mackie.
cavalry being always here till the new barracks
were erected at Windsor. The "Bear" accommodated the officers, the non-commissioners officers
put up at the "Bull," and the rank and file
were distributed amongst the other inns. Out- Mackie. Cox.
side each public-house was a "soldiers' room,"
with a ladder, or steps, leading to it. Such
rooms and steps, or their remains, were visible
in some cases as late as the beginning of the
twentieth century.

It was at the "Bear" that the memorable
interview took place between King James I. and
the Vicar of Bray.

The story goes that in the reign of King
James I., the king, hunting with the buckhounds, lost his way and came quite alone into
the yard of the "Bear." He instantly asked
what he could have for dinner: the reply was
rather laconic—"Nothing, sir; it is Lent, and
all the fish is bespoke, and dressing for dinner
for the Vicar of Bray and his curate." The
King said, "Go up to them, and say that there
is a gentleman here who gives his humble service
to them, and would be much obliged to them if
they would give him leave to dine with them."
His Majesty was asked to walk up, and they
soon entered into conversation. The dinner
passed off very pleasantly. At length the
reckoning was to be called for. When it arrived
the King said, "Gentlemen, I know not what
to do; I left home in haste, and forgot to take
any money in my pocket, and am really without
a shilling." "A pretty fellow, indeed!" to

come and get a dinner from us in this way!
No, no; you must settle it with the landlord.
I'll not pay for your dinner, I promise you."
The curate said, "Oh, sir, do not speak thus
to the gentleman; I'll pay his reckoning, and
think myself well repaid for his entertaining
conversation." The King thanked the curate,
and said he certainly would repay him. Scarce
was this conversation over, when a great noise
was heard in the "Bear" yard; horns blowing,
lords, gentlemen, yeomen, etc. "Has anything
been heard of His Majesty? Has he passed
through here?" His Majesty opened the balcony
door and presented himself. Instantly there
were one hundred bent knees. The poor Vicar
then bent his knee, and begged pardon. "Did
not know it was His Majesty, or —— " His
Majesty replied, "Oh, mon! I forgive you; you
shall be Vicar of Bray still, I promise you, and"
turning to his friend the curate, " as there is a
Canonry of Windsor now vacant, you, mon, shall
have it."

In 1489, an inn called "the Swan" was in
existence, but as it stood in the parish of Bray,
it cannot have been one with the house bearing
that sign to-day, the present "Swan" being in
the ancient parish of Cookham. The record is
brief, but strengthens the idea that Maidenhead
inn-keepers made hay when the sun shone.
"Richard Hithe holds an inn called the 'Swan,'
and sells victuals and takes excessive gain."

B. C. R. and
Kerry 145.

B. C. R.

The "White Horse" must have existed as
an inn from at least the time of Elizabeth,
as on 17th April, 36 Eliz: (1574) Richard

Wormistone, of Maidenhead, innholder, sold the property to Richard Winch.

The " Greyhound " may or may not have been more ancient than the other inns. It was, however, not only one of the chief houses in the town, but grew to be one of the best on the Bath Road, if not in all England. Here it was that King Charles I. and his children partook of refreshment on the occasion of their memorable last interview on 16th July, 1647, and here, too, Thomas Ellwood was detained, as described in another chapter. It stood on the north side of the High Street and its site is now occupied by No. 66. It was unfortunately entirely destroyed by fire. The Northampton Mercury, 22nd March, 1735-6, thus records the calamity :—

" Last Saturday Night the Greyhound Inn at Maidenhead was burned down to the Ground, and out of the 36 Standing Beds, &c., only three Feather Beds and one Pewter Dish was saved, even all the Plate, Money, and Books were lost ; it was accounted one of the best furnished inns in England. It began in the Maid's Apartment ; Mr. Freeman and his Wife who kept the Inn, were in London to prove a Will ; since their Return the Servants have been kept in Custody, to see what Discoveries can be made." ^{Kingston's Hist. Wycombe. p. 187.}

Kingston's Hist. Wycombe. p. 187.

In 1652 there existed an inn bearing the sign of " St. George and the Dragon," and preserved in the local museum is a token of that date with a George and Dragon on one side, the letters R. E. D. on the other side and the legend " At . the . George . In . in . Mayden Head 1652."

Both the " Saracen's Head," the " Lion,"
and the " Sun " certainly go back to the days
of Charles II., and probably earlier. The "Lion"
figures in the Bridgemasters' Accounts for 8th
June, 1663, " Paid Goody Milton at the Bridge
for bread and beer when the perambulation was
gone 3s. 4d. Paid same day at the ' Lion ' for
bread and beer and wine 13s. 4d." In 1807 the
Excise Office was at the " Lion."

Crossby's
Gazetteer.

The " Sun " was a vast place standing at the
corner of Castle Hill and Marlow Road, and
having the ground on the South side of the road
just opposite for its gardens. A curiously trained
tree still stands on the boundary line of two of
these properties, the tree being the old arbour
of ancient days.

Amongst the other inns were the " Fighting
Cocks," under and at back of the Town Hall;
the " Fox and Horn," now the " Crown "; the
"King's Arms," a large and well-known house
near the west end of Maidenhead Bridge on
north side; the " White Hart," now shops of
the Crescet Tower, High Street; the "Fleece,"
now the " Windsor Castle "; the " Quart Pot,"
now the " Coronation "; the " Maidenhead,"
now the " Criterion," High Street, and others.

On the top of Castle Hill stood the " Folly,"
down to 1820 almost the last house on the west
side of the town, as is shown in Alderman
Silver's " Map of Maidenhead," preserved in
the local Public Library. Its name has given
rise to some conjecture, though it is not quite
an uncommon name, being, as Money states in
his History of Newbury, one of those words

constantly observed along the lines of Roman ways. Lowsley states that "Volly," the Berkshire equivalent for Folly, indicates a circular group of fir trees on the crest of a hill. This house certainly occupied the crest of a hill universally known down to the end of the first half of the nineteenth century, as Folly Hill. So far back, however, as 1682, Richard Cook erected certain structures on this site that gained for themselves the name of "Cook's Folly," as is witnessed by one of the title deeds of the present "Windsor Castle" inn, bearing date 15th March, 3 James II., and being a conveyance from Stephen Morris to William Collett.

On the extreme east of the town there stands an inn widely known as "Skindle's," formerly the "Orkney Arms," and though only a part of it is in the Borough of Maidenhead it must not be omitted in this notice, for many a time has the mace gone in at a door and out of a window on occasions of beating the bounds. Here dwelt in 1736 a landlord to whom some would-be wit of the time addressed the following lines :—

> " Friend Isaac, 'tis strange you that live so near Bray
> Should not set up the sign of ' *the Vicar* ';
> Though it may be an odd one, you cannot but say
> It must needs be a sign of good liquor."

" Friend Isaac," was, however, quite equal to the occasion, and promptly responded.

> " Indeed, master poet, your reason's but poor,
> For the Vicar would think it a sin
> To stay like a booby and lounge at the door;
> 'Twere a sign of bad liquor within."

"Skindle's" may easily be located in Turner's great picture, " Rain, Steam, and Speed." The railway is the Great Western, and the bridge is

Brunel's great work, here spanning the river Thames.

At this same "Skindle's"—"Orkney Arms" in those days—dwelt the landlord of whom James Payn tells a good story, quoted in Tristram's "Coaching Days and Coaching Ways." Mine host was a Whig, and boasted he had always twelve votes at his command. To him came a Tory lawyer, on election business bent, and put up at his house. Having to go to London for the munitions of war, he was, on his return with a very large sum of "munitions," stopped on Hounslow Heath by the landlord's scapegrace son. The man of law, however, managed to escape, and arrived at the Orkney Arms in due course, "munitions" and all. In a private conversation with the landlord he told how someone had attempted highway robbery on him, and suggested that before more was said the landlord might have a little talk with his son. He did so, and returning with a very rueful countenance, asked what the lawyer was going to do. "Nothing to injure an old friend," was the answer, " provided ——! " and so it came to pass, somehow, that all those twelve voters went Tory on that election.

To these various inns came all sorts and conditions of men in all sorts and conditions of vehicles. First and foremost came the mail and stage coaches. The mails, as their name indicates, carried the letters, and they were exempt from toll. In 1787 there were eight mail coaches passing over Maidenhead Bridge every day toll-free. The total number of mail and

Bridge
M. & C.
p. 166.

stage coaches passing through the town daily is not easy to decide. In the absence of definite documentary evidence, reliance must be placed on those whose memory carries them back to 1830 or so. Mr. Richard Silver and Mr. Robert Walker have both stated to the writer that the number was ninety. To these must be added the post chaises, which were a sort of large brougham, and all the other varieties of vehicle which flourished before railways or motor-cars were thought of. Then, too, there were the waggons, many of which were exceedingly heavy, with wheel-tyres nine inches broad. They were the steam rollers of those days, and as there was no other way of rolling in the stones than by the traffic over them, these broad-wheeled waggons were encouraged by being exempt from toll. In fact, for waggons the scale of tolls was regulated by the breadth of the tyre. As the High Street was paved with cobble stones from the top of the town to the Chapel Arches, it may well be believed that the noise and racket were frightful both by day and by night. It was Mr. Higgs, the Surveyor, who brought in a better state of affairs. He took up all the cobbles, removed them to the meadow by the Chapel Arches, broke them up, and re-laid them. Blessings on his memory!

The convenient distance of Maidenhead from the Metropolis often made it the first stopping-place in journeys and expeditions to the West.

Thus, on 25th August, 1663, the Earl of Anglesey writes to the Marquis of Ormond that " His Majesty (Ch. II.) and the Queen go

Silver. MSS. of Marquis of Ormond, Br. Mus.

to-morrow as far as Maidenhead towards the bath."

So also in an interesting paper describing Lord Feversham's progress from London to the close of the battle of Sedgemoor in connection with the rising of the Duke of Monmouth, it is said, "On Saturday, 20th June, 1685, the Earl of Feversham, His Majestie's Lieut. General with 150 guards and 60 granadeers marched from London to Maidenhead."

George Selwyn, also, writing under date of 23rd July, 1774, to Lord Carlisle, says, "I sup to-night at March's with the Essex's; they go to-morrow on a party to Slough and Maiden-bridge [sic]."

So also Mrs. Philip Lybbe Powys writes in 1760, "We once more bid adieu to the Metropolis. Our first day's place of breakfasting was the Orkney Arms, Maidenhead Bridge."

And there was another reason for stopping at Maidenhead—Maidenhead Thicket! This notorious shelter of highwaymen and footpads was far pleasanter to cross by day than by night, and its vicinity doubtless caused many a traveller, as he saw the shades of evening gather, to think he had gone far enough for one day. This was evidently the view taken by Lord

Bruce, who, writing on 7th December, 1793, to his father, the Earl of Aylesbury, says, "I think Lord Elgin had a most fortunate escape from the footpads that attacked him on Maiden-head Thicket. That serves as a lesson not to travel of a night, particularly in our country." It is, however, said that travellers from the

West were the victims preferred, those coming from London having been previously dealt with on Hounslow Heath!

It is vain to speculate on the names or numbers of those who have made Maidenhead their halting place. Lying as it does on a main road from London to the West, thousands of well-known personages have either halted for refreshment or broken their journey here. James First's encounter with the Vicar of Bray has been already mentioned. Charles I. must have come more than once, for not only was his sad last interview with his children here, but on 9th November, 1642, he wrote from Maidenhead to the Mayor of Exeter, charging him to apprehend all persons raising levies without permission. One visit of Charles II. has been noted above. He passed through the town again in 1665, as the Bridgemasters' Accounts show, for the Corporation indulged in a dinner which cost £1 15s. od., and they gave another £1 to his Majesty's footmen.

MSS. of Duke of Portland, Br. Mus.

Maid. I. 65, p. 19.

In September, 1686, an order was issued for a troop to march to Maidenhead "to conduct our dearest sister, the Queen Dowager (the widow of Charles II.) from there to Reading." It is not absolutely certain that William III. passed through Maidenhead on his march to London, but it is in the highest degree probable that he came through with his troops. In 1787 George III. and the whole of the royal family attended Maidenhead races. On Wednesday, 4th August, 1809, Queen Charlotte, the Duke of Cambridge, and the Princesses Augusta,

MSS. of Lord Montague, Br. Mus.

V. C. H. II. 308.

Rutland.

Sophia, Elizabeth, and Mary paid a visit to Cliveden, the royal party being conveyed by boats from Maidenhead Bridge to the landing place, where they were received by Lady Orkney and a large company of nobility and gentry, vast crowds lining the river banks. On 29th April, 1805, the Duke of Cambridge reviewed the Berkshire County Volunteer Corps on Maidenhead Thicket. Queen Victoria and King Edward VII. have both paid many visits to Cliveden and Taplow Court, and passed through the town on their various journeys. On one of these King Edward had a narrow escape from being stopped by the policeman on point duty for not having a number on his motor-car. In the nick of time a fortunate observance of the royal arms saved both His Majesty and the guardian of the peace from an unfortunate contretemps.

In addition to these royal personages, mention may perhaps be made of Pepys, who came through the town for the first time on 17th June, 1668, having " set out with one coach in company, and through Maydenhead which I never saw before to Colebrook by noon; the way mighty good "; and also of those of whom Shakespeare tells in the "Merry Wives," Act 4, Scene 5 : " There is a friend of mine come to town, tells me there is three couzin germans, that has cozened all the hosts of Reading, of Maidenhead, of Colebrook, of horses and money."

As a matter of fact they were the Duke of Wurtemberg and his suite, to whom, as royal guests, were given special facilities along the roads, which facilities they grossly abused, using up so many horses that ordinary travellers were greatly inconvenienced.

The visit of the Eton boys, too, must not be forgotten. In November, 1768, a rebellion broke out at Eton College in the VIth and Upper Vth Forms respecting the right of the assistant masters to send back to college such præpostors as were found out of bounds. Some 160 boys were implicated, of whom a very considerable number " took boats "—so it is said—came to Maidenhead, and stayed all night, running up a bill for £55 18s. 3d. at Marsh's Inn by the Bridge. Yet, as Rutland observes, " £56 for a day and a half of good living, with abundance of beer, wine, punch, &c., for 160 growing boys does not seem an exorbitant charge, and those who know the scale on which a modern inn-keeper's bill at the same river-side town is generally estimated must sigh for a return of the ancient charges."

Maxwell Lyte's Hist. Eton Coll.

M.F.C. 1890-1. p. 56.

The original bill is preserved in the possession of Sir J. W. Buchannan Riddell. It is endorsed, " Bill at Maidenhead Bridge for the entertainment of the boys concerned in the Eton Rebellion 2nd November, 1768." The following are the items. :—

	£	s.	d.
Beer for dinner	1	2	6
Wine & punch, &c.	6	18	6
Dinners, coffee, tea, &c., suppers and breakfast for 160 at 5s. per head ...	40	0	0
Beer at Supper	0	18	6
Wine and punch	5	14	9
Fires	1	0	0
Cards	0	4	0

November the 2nd & 3rd, 1768. £55 18 3

Many of the boys went next day to their homes. Amongst these was William Grenville, a future Prime Minister, whose father promptly sent him back to the college to be flogged and removed. Of his brother it is recorded that when before the secession all the older boys threw their books into the river, ' Thomas Grenville would not part with his Homer.'

The Etonians used also to visit Maidenhead on their Montem Day. Two representatives of the College arrayed in velvet doublets and other old-fashioned costume were posted on Maidenhead Bridge, and there, as at Salt Hill, demanded " Salt " from all who passed by, the proceeds being devoted to the maintenance of a scholar at

Silver.

Cambridge. Mr. Richard Silver well remembers being stopped with his father on Maidenhead Bridge with the usual adjuration, " Custom, not law."

Thomas Ellwood's visit will claim a chapter to itself.

" At Cheltenham Spa." Humphries & Willoughby.

On the 13th June, 1785, Warren Hastings landed from India, and at once sent a message to his wife, then staying at Cheltenham, to meet him on Maidenhead Bridge. Two days later a most affectionate meeting took place, though the probability is that the meeting was actually in the " Orkney Arms," which stood next to the bridge on the Bucks side, and was widely known and patronised as a large and first-class hotel.

Boaden's Life of Mrs. Jordan.

In 1811 another meeting took place on the same spot, but, alas! of a widely different character. Mrs. Jordan, who had given herself whole-heartedly to the Duke of Clarence, was

gracing the stage at Cheltenham, when just
before the performance she received a heartless
letter from the Duke requiring her to meet him
at Maidenhead Bridge, and dismissing her. She
persisted in playing, for it was her friend
Watson's benefit. She struggled on with her
part—Nell, in "The Devil to Pay,"—till Jobson
had to accuse her of being "laughing" drunk.
Poor Nell tried to laugh, but became hysterical,
when Jobson at once said "crying" drunk,
thus covering her distress. After the performance she was at once put into a travelling chariot
in her stage dress to keep her appointment with
the Royal Duke, in a state of anguish easier to
conceive than to describe.

Of lesser lights it is impossible to speak, but
there was a section of the community who used
to pass through Maidenhead in the beginning of
the last century who claim a brief notice. These
were the Irish labourers, who, coming over
to England for harvesting, were in the habit
of settling themselves in various parishes
and becoming a considerable burden to the
authorities. Those near London solved the
difficulty by passing them on to Bristol, and
thence to Ireland. The labourers were conveyed
stage by stage in Pass-Carts, two-wheeled, one   Silver.
horse vehicles, carrying 6 or 8 people. Colnbrook was one of these stages and Maidenhead
was the next. Arrived here, they might either
spend the night at a lodging house, or doss down
at the "Pass-on," a wooden lean-to structure,
the remains of which were still to be seen as
late as 1920 in the rear of No. 100 High Street,

and the "Criterion." But those who had money preferred to go on towards Boyn Hill and patronise Mother Greengrass, whose "hotel" was as well known as her tongue was fluent and her vocabulary rich. It is said she got behind once with her rent, and a certain young gentleman, who afterwards achieved civic distinction, was sent to distrain on her pig. As he bent to seize the porker, a pail of hot water descended and scalded off the whiskers from one side of his face. It was long before he forgot either the hot water or Mother Greengrass' eloquence.

Bridge, M. & C.

An entry in the Bridge Accounts for 12th October, 1826, seems to infer that the Pass-cart was superseded about that time. " Paid James Frowd four quarters' allowances in lieu of the emoluments arising from conveying vagrants due at Michs. last £8."

CHAPTER XII.

THOMAS ELLWOOD AT MAIDENHEAD.

THOMAS ELLWOOD was the son of an Oxfordshire Justice of the Peace residing at Crowell, a little village nestling at the foot of the Chilterns, not a great way from Watlington. Towards the end of the Commonwealth days Ellwood joined the Society of Friends, and the account of his life written by himself has become an English classic.

Early one Sunday morning in the spring of 1660, having promised to attend a meeting at Chalfont St. Giles, in Buckinghamshire, he set off from Reading, where he then was, and in due time arrived at Maidenhead. Now the Quakers were much less strict about Sabbath observance than the Puritans, and it never for a moment entered the head of Ellwood that he would give offence by riding his horse through Maidenhead on the Lord's day. The good people of this town thought otherwise, and what followed must be given in Ellwood's own words :—

"The watchman, laying hold on the bridle, told me I must go with him to the constable; and accordingly I, making no resistance, suffered him to lead my horse to the constable's door. When we were come there the constable told me I must go before the warden, who was the chief officer of that town, and bade the watchman bring me on, himself walking before.

Hist. of Thomas Ellwood. p. 69 in Morley's Universal Library.

" Being come to the warden's door, the
constable knocked, and desired to speak with
Mr. Warden. He thereupon quickly coming to
the door, the constable said : 'Sir, I have brought
a man here to you whom the watch took riding
through the town.' The warden was a budge
old man ; and I looked somewhat big too, having
a good gelding under me, and a good riding-coat
on my back, both which my friend Isaac Pening-
ton had kindly accommodated me with for that
journey.

" The warden therefore taking me to be (as
the saying is) somebody, put off his hat and made
a low congée to me ; but when he saw that I sat
still, and neither bowed to him nor moved my
hat, he gave a start, and said to the constable :
' You said you had brought a man, but he don't
behave like a man.'

" I sat still upon my horse and said not a
word, but kept my mind retired to the Lord,
waiting to see what this would come to.

" The warden then began to examine me,
asking me whence I came and whither I was
going ; I told him I came from Reading and was
going to Chalfont. He asked me why I did
travel on that day. I told him I did not know
that it would give any offence barely to ride or
to walk on that day, so long as I did not carry
or drive any carriage or horses laden with
burthens. ' Why,' said he, ' if your business
was urgent, did you not take a pass from the
mayor of Reading ? ' ' Because,' I replied, ' I
did not know nor think I should have needed
one.' ' Well,' said he, ' I will not talk with you

now, because it is time to go to church, but I
will examine you further anon.' And turning
to the constable, ' Have him,' said he, ' to an
inn, and bring him before me after dinner.'

" The naming of an inn put me in mind that
such public-houses were places of expense, and I
knew I had no money to defray it; wherefore I
said to the Warden : ' Before thou sendest me
to an inn, which may occasion some expense,
I think it needful to acquaint thee that I have
no money.'

" At that the warden started again, and
turning quickly upon me, said : ' How! no
money! How can that be? You don't look like
a man that has no money.' ' However I look,'
said I, ' I tell thee the truth, that I have no
money; and I tell it to forewarn thee, that thou
mayest not bring any charge upon the town.'
' I wonder,' said he, 'what art you have got, that
you can travel without money; you can do more,
I assure you, than I can.'

" I making no answer, he went on and said :
' Well! but if you have no money, you have a
good horse under you, and we can distrain him
for the charge.' ' But,' said I, ' the horse is
not mine.' ' No,' said he, ' but you have a good
coat on your back, and that I hope is your own.'
' No,' said I, ' but it is not, for I borrowed both
the horse and the coat.'

" With that the warden, holding up his hands
and smiling, said : ' Bless me! I never met with
such a man as you are before. What! were you
set out by the parish?' Then, turning to the
constable, he said : ' Have him to the Grey-

hound, and bid the people be civil to him.'
Accordingly, to the Greyhound I was led, my
horse set up, and I put into a large room, and
some account, I suppose, given of me to the
people of the house.

" This was new work to me, and what the
issue of it would be I could not foresee ; but being
left there alone, I sat down, and retired in spirit
to the Lord, in whom alone my strength and
safety were, and begged support of Him ; even
that He would be pleased to give me wisdom and
words to answer the warden when I should come
to be examined again before him.

" After some time, having pen, ink, and paper
about me, I set myself to write what I thought
might be proper, if occasion served, to give the
warden ; and while I was writing, the master of
the house, being come home from his worship,
sent the tapster to me to invite me to dine with
him. I bid him tell his master that I had not
any money to pay for my dinner. He sent the
man again to tell me I should be welcome to
dine with him though I had no money. I desired
him to tell his master ' that I was very sensible
of his civility and kindness in so courteously
inviting me to his table, but I had not freedom
to eat of his meat unless I could have paid for
it.' So he went on with his dinner, and I with
my writing.

" But before I had finished what was on my
mind to write, the constable came again, bring-
ing with him his fellow-constable. This was a
brisk, genteel young man, a shopkeeper in the
town, whose name was Cherry. They saluted

me very civilly, and told me they were come to have me before the warden. This put an end to my writing, which I put into my pocket, and went along with them.

"Being come to the warden's, he asked me again the same questions he had asked me before; to which I gave him the like answers. Then he told me the penalty I had incurred, which he said was either to pay so much money or lie so many hours in the stocks, and asked me which I would choose; I replied, 'I shall not choose either. And,' said I, 'I have told thee already that I have no money; though if I had, I could not so far acknowledge myself an offender as to pay any. But as to lying in the stocks, I am in thy power, to do unto me what it shall please the Lord to suffer thee.'

"When he heard that he paused awhile, and then he told me, 'He considered that I was but a young man, and might not perhaps understand the danger I had brought myself into, and therefore he would not use the severity of the law upon me; but, in hopes that I would be wiser hereafter, he would pass by this offence and discharge me.'

"Then putting on a countenance of the greatest gravity, he said to me, 'But, young man, I would have you know that you have not only broken the law of the land, but the law of God also; and therefore you ought to ask His forgiveness, for you have highly offended Him.' 'That,' said I, 'I would most willingly do if I were sensible that in this case I had offended Him by breaking any law of His.' 'Why,' said

he, ' do you question that ! ' ' Yes, truly,' said
I, ' for I do not know that any law of God doth
forbid me to ride on this day.' ' No ! ' said he;
' that's strange. Where, I wonder, was you
bred? You can read, can't you ? ' ' Yes,' said
I, ' that I can.' ' Don't you then read,' said
he, ' the commandment, " Remember the Sabbath day to keep it holy. Six days shalt thou
labour and do all thy work; but the seventh day
is the Sabbath of the Lord; in it thou shalt not
do any work."? ' ' Yes,' I replied, ' I have
both read it often, and remember it very well.
But that command was given to the Jews, not to
Christians; and this is not that day, for that
was the seventh day, but this is the first.'
' How,' said he, ' do you know the days of the
week no better? You had need then be better
taught.'

" Here the younger constable, whose name
was Cherry, interposing, said : ' Mr. Warden,
the gentleman is in the right as to that, for this
is the first day of the week, and not the seventh.'

" This the old warden took in dungeon, and
looking severely on the constable, said : 'What !
do you take upon you to teach me? I'll have
you know I will not be taught by you." ' As
you please for that, sir,' said the constable; 'but
I am sure you are mistaken in this point; for
Saturday I know is the seventh day, and you
know yesterday was Saturday.'

" This made the warden hot and testy, and
put him almost out of all patience, so that I
feared it would have come to a downright quarrel
betwixt them, for both were confident and neither

would yield; and so earnestly were they engaged
in the contest, that there was no room for me
to put in a word between them.

"At length the old man, having talked himself out of wind, stood still awhile as it were to
take breath, and then bethinking himself of me,
he turned to me and said : ' You are discharged,
and may take your liberty to go about your
occasions.' ' But,' said I, ' I desire my horse
may be discharged too, else I know not how to
go.' ' Ay, ay,' said he, ' you shall have your
horse,' and turning to the other constable, who
had not offended him, he said : ' Go, see that
his horse be delivered to him.'

"Away thereupon went I with that constable,
leaving the old warden and the young constable
to compose their differences as they could.
Being come to the inn, the constable called for my
horse to be brought out; which done, I
immediately mounted, and began to set forward.
But the hostler, not knowing the condition of
my pocket, said modestly to me : ' Sir, don't you
forget to pay for your horse's standing ? ' ' No,
truly,' said I, ' I don't forget it; but I have no
money to pay it with, and so I told the warden
before.' ' Well, hold your tongue,' said the
constable 'to the hostler; ' I'll see you paid.'
Then opening the gate, they let me out, the
constable wishing me a good journey, and through
the town I rode without further molestation,
though it was as much sabbath, I thought, when
I went out as it was when I came in.''

CHAPTER XIII.

ECCLESIASTICAL.

CHURCH OF ENGLAND.

FOR five hundred and eighty-five years prior to 1855 one building had sufficed for the spiritual necessities of the members of the Anglican Communion in Maidenhead. The next fifty years saw the erection of five new churches, of which the first, and in many ways the most important was All Saints', Boyne Hill. It was erected largely through the munificence of the daughter of the Rev. William Hulme, Incumbent of Holy Trinity, Reading, from designs by Mr. Geo. E. Street, R.A., and on land given by Mr. Charles Grenfell. The foundation stone was laid on 23rd October, 1855, by Bishop Wilberforce, of Oxford, who also consecrated the building on 2nd December, 1857. This Church marked a distinct stage in English ecclesiastical architecture, and it was said at the time that there were "few churches so original in character, so effective in design, and so perfect in every detail." Adjoining the Church are vicarage, clergy house, schools, and alms houses, and in the centre of a quadrangle rises a large ornamental Cross. The tower and spire were erected in 1866-7, and in the following year a fire destroyed the bells, which were, however, speedily replaced. A handsome memorial brass in the chancel floor commemorates the first Vicar, the Rev. William Gresley, whose " Siege of Lichfield,'" " Forest of Arden," and other works of fiction had a very considerable success on their first appearance. Mr. Gresley was also the author of several theological works. He was a prebend of Lichfield, and a man of considerable influence in the Church of England. He died 19th November, 1876, and was succeeded by the Rev. A. H. Drummond, Honorary Canon of Christ Church, Oxford, the Rev. W. A. Thackeray, and the Rev. W. S. Mahony.

St. Luke's was the next Church to make its appearance. It was consecrated by Bishop Wilberforce of Oxford, on 23rd August, 1866, enlarged in 1869, and in 1894 its beautifully proportioned and graceful spire was added from the designs of Mr. J. Oldred Scott. St. Luke's was created a District Chapelry, or ecclesiastical parish, out of the Parish of Cookham, on 1st March, 1867. Its first Vicar was the Rev. W. B. Hole, who was succeeded in 1874 by the Rev. W. G. Sawyer, in 1890 by the Rev. H. G. J. Meara, and in 1914 by the Rev. C. E. M. Fry, who is also the Rural Dean.

Nat. Sch. Charity Deed.

St. Paul's, in Hightown Road, and St. Peter's, at the Furze Plat, were both designed by Mr. E. J. Shrewsbury. St. Paul's is a chapel-of-ease to All Saints', and was consecrated on 4th November, 1889, by Bishop Stubbs.

St. Peter's was consecrated on 14th April, 1898, as a chapel-of-ease to St. Luke's. Ten years afterwards it was considerably enlarged, being re-opened on 21st October, 1908. On 6th

Feb., 1928, the surrounding district was gazetted a separate parish.

St. Mark's is the Church of the Poor Law Institution, but has constantly attracted a congregation from outside. It was designed by Mr. Charles Cooper, and was presented to the Guardians by Mr. John Hibbert of Braywick in 1873, then and for many years Chairman of the Board.

CONGREGATIONAL.

In 1662 nearly two thousand clergymen of the Church of England were ejected from their livings for refusing to conform to the provisions of the Act of Uniformity, then recently passed. Though it cannot be absolutely stated that one of these ejected ministers was the founder of the Maidenhead Congregational Church, there is little doubt it came into existence as the direct result of that cruel piece of persecution. The Rev. William Brice, ejected from his rectory at Henley-on-Thames, came of a family owning land in Maidenhead, and ten years after the Act of Uniformity was residing here on his own estate. He was without any pastoral charge, though he frequently preached both in Maidenhead and other places. His son was the Rev. John Brice, who on his ejectment from East-hampstead rectory settled in Dover, and it is believed to be his name which appears on the earliest trust deed of the Maidenhead Congregational Chapel. It is a lease for 99 years from "John Brice of Dover, Clerk," to Messrs. Keene

CONGREGATIONAL CHURCH—1785.

and others, bearing date 1696. But by 1712 a congregation of 200 had been gathered together under the pastoral care of Richard Stretton. Mr. Stretton's father, who bore the same name, had been ejected from his position as Assistant to Dr. Cheynel, of Petwell, Sussex, and, as he was noted for the interest he took in "poor country congregations," it is by no means improbable that he was the real founder of the local Church. In 1784 the congregation was assembling in a building in Market Street, which has been successively a chapel, a private school, and the "Hope" public-house. In this year, on April 6th, the Rev. John Cooke commenced his ministrations here. Under his long and influential pastorate of forty-three years Congregationalism assumed an assured position, preaching stations were established in Burnham, Littlewick, and many neighbouring villages, and the small meeting house in Market Street was exchanged for the commodious building with its adjacent burial-ground in West Street—then known as Back Lane. The building was opened on 18th September, 1785, free of debt. It had a flat ceiling, the gallery was supported with heavy wooden posts, and the pews were high enough for the children to sleep in them without being seen. It was lighted with candles, which were snuffed by an official who went round for that purpose during the singing. In the gallery, opposite each light, was placed a pair of snuffers, the person sitting nearest being supposed to keep his candle snuffed.

The Corporation muniments record that the

Silver.

Maid. R. 194.

new Chapel was "registered on 8th April, 1785, as a place of worship on a requisition signed by John Cooke, John Langton, Stephen Westbrook, and Joseph Trone," and on the same day it is further recorded that the "Rev. John Cooke took the oath of allegiance as required by protestant dissenting ministers." Mr. Cooke, who had been a school teacher at Wooburn in his youth, was a man of dignified presence, dauntless courage and inflexible principle, and the events of his life gave him ample opportunity of putting to the proof all three of these qualities. His encounter with a regimental officer whom he compelled to apologise for breaking his windows illustrated the first; his fearless facing of a crowd who attacked him at Burnham with lighted straw previously dipped in pitch proved the second; and his opposition to certain forms of amusement with which it was proposed to celebrate the jubilee of George III. testified to the third, and brought down on him that deluge of abuse, part of which may still be studied in a volume entitled "The Saints of Maidenhead," in the local Public Library. Mr. Cooke was a distinct personality in his day, and no history of Maidenhead would be complete which did not make some reference to this able and faithful man of God. He died 19th October, 1826. The work Mr. Cooke did so much to strengthen and consolidate still prospers, though modern methods have taken the place of older ones. Candles have made way for a more brilliant illuminant; an organ accompanies the service of song which once was led by flute, fiddle, viola, clarionet, 'cello, bassoon, and double bass; and Sunday Scholars are no longer assembled on a Good Friday to be regaled with a cake, and that "mug of beer" which good old Mr. Langton used generously to supply from his neighbouring brewery in "the good old days."

COUNTESS OF HUNTINGDON'S CONNEXION.

The Rev. John Cooke, the Congregational pastor of whom mention has been made, doubtless had the defects of his qualities, as have most other people, and some of his flock thought he was given to rule matters with too heavy a hand. They even went so far as to suggest to him the desirability of his seeking another sphere of usefulness, and when he very naturally declined to avail himself of the suggestion they resigned membership on 22nd May, 1815, took rooms at the "White Hart," High Street, now the Crescet Tower, and opened them as a place of worship, celebrating the proceedings with an opening dinner which the minute books say cost £9.

A building in White Hart Lane was either erected or adapted for services, and opened in the following October, the collections at the opening services amounting to the substantial sum of £102 17s. 7d. The first regular pastor was the Rev. Griffith Davies Owen, a man of a beautiful spirit, who on Christmas Day, 1815, commenced a pastorate only terminated by his death in 1836. The tradition of the "opening dinner" was regularly maintained, and at the yearly anniversary certain leading men of the congregation, numbering about twenty-six, were accustomed to dine together at the "White Hart." In 1829 the ladies desired to join them, but after solemn consultation it was decided by the lords of creation not to depart from the usual procedure, as there were "many insurmountable objections." In 1841 the congregation moved to a new Chapel at the corner of High Street and Windsor Road, which was occupied till the denomination discontinued its services in 1858, and sold the building to the Wesleyan Methodists.

BAPTISTS.

Tenison, MS. 639.

In a return of "Conventicles" presented to Archbishop Sheldon in 1669, there appears the following entry :—

Cookham—1 Conventicle.

At ye houses of Nath : Rich, Esquire ; Peter Darval, Miller ; James Jeffrey ; William Jerome ; and Lawrence Jessy—by turnes

Sect—

Number—not a few.

Qualitie—some of indifferent good estate.

Heads and Teachers—Nath : Rich, aforesd., Col. of 2 Regiments horse and Dragoons in ye late Rebellion ; William Rutledge, Mealman ; Wm. Jerome ; Peter Dervall ; and Edward Gillett of Bray, Collar Maker.

St. Pap. Dom.

That these men were Baptists, and also Maidenhead Baptists, appears from an entry in the State Papers of Charles II., being a record of applications for Preaching Licenses under the Royal Indulgence of 1672.

Given in by Mr. Blood, 18th April, 1672—

Will. Rutledg, of Maydenhead, in ye County of Berks, teacher among ye people called Baptists, and ye people with him, desire that they may be allowed to meet in James Jeffrey's house in ye parish of Cookham in ye sd. County.

Edward Gillett, of Maydenhead, teacher among ye like people, desires yt he and ye people with him, may be allowed to meete at James Jeffrey's house in Cookham aforesd.

Throughout the above Bray and Cookham mean Bray parish and Cookham parish, and it will be noted that both the " teachers " reside in Maidenhead. Beyond these entries no record has yet come to light as to the success or failure of these men, their progress or persecutions. But knowing as we do how full the jails at Reading and Aylesbury were of men whose only crime was nonconformity, it is but reasonable to suppose that even in Maidenhead the Baptists did not find matters a bed of roses.

In 1778 the Baptists of Maidenhead were connected with Reading, and regarded as members of the Reading King's Road Particular

Baptist Church residing at a distance. They had
no separate organised church in their own town,
though they doubtless met together for worship,
but calls to the ministry and other ecclesiastical
functions were exercised at Reading. Thus on
13th April, 1778, Mr. William Burnham, though
a Maidenhead man, was summoned to Reading
to exercise his gifts before the King's Road
Church, that they might judge whether or no
he were qualified to receive the ministerial call.
It is on record that he preached four sermons,
three times from selected texts, but on the first
occasion as a favour he was allowed to choose
his own topic. These and other tests proving
satisfactory, Mr. Burnham received the " right
hand of fellowship " on 14th August following.
He was now recognised as a regular pastor, and
there is reason to believe that for some years
Maidenhead was the chief sphere of his labours.

Between this date and the beginning of the
nineteenth century theological differences made
themselves apparent in the various Baptist
Churches, but how far these affected Maidenhead is not known. All that can be said is, that
in 1847 the only organised congregation of
Baptists in Maidenhead consisted of those whose
rigid adherence to the tenets of John Calvin had
earned for them the title of Strict Baptists. Of
these a little company was meeting regularly in
a room over Messrs. Fuller's granary in Market
Street, when they were joined in that year by
Mr. Julius Neve, who had recently come from
his native County of Kent to settle in Maidenhead. The granary room proving inconvenient,

Mr. Neve placed his drawing room at No. 57 High Street at the disposal of the congregation, who worshipped there till 1856, when they occupied the school room of a private school which was carried on first in King Street and subsequently in York Road, and here a church was formally constituted in 1860. The dispersal of the Countess of Huntingdon's Congregation in 1858 brought some accession of numbers; the school room proved too small. A new home was found in a Chapel in York Road, which was erected through the generosity of Mr. Neve, and opened on the 25th January, 1865.

In addition to the Strict Baptists there were other Baptists who were unable to take up such a strong calvinistic position as their brethren, and these had for a long time found their home with the Congregationalists. But as the town grew and population increased, it was not unnatural that those who adhered to believers' baptism should consider whether their numbers did not justify the formation of a separate organisation. A suitable opportunity for so doing occurred in 1871, and the present church was erected in Marlow Road, at a cost of £1,020, from designs by Mr. C. A. Vardy, the congregation temporarily occupying the Town Hall while the building was in progress. The opening took place on Sunday, 25th May, 1873, and on the following Tuesday two services were conducted by that celebrated Baptist preacher, the Rev. C. H. Spurgeon, the vast crowds who gathered to hear him being accommodated in a huge marquee in Kidwell's Park, there being no building in the town large enough to hold them. Mr. Spurgeon preached from a waggon, and the evening discourse was of a distinctly "popular" character. But the present writer, who occupied a seat in the waggon during the sermon, will never forget the few words the great preacher addressed to him afterwards, manifesting as they did in a striking way Mr. Spurgeon's eager, almost anxious desire that the service should prove of value in the highest and most spiritual sense.

SOCIETY OF FRIENDS.

Scattered notices of Maidenhead in the literature of the Society of Friends indicate that some members of that community have dwelt in the town or exercised a passing ministry in it almost from the time when Halhead and Salthouse came to Reading in 1665, which is the earliest record of Quakerism in this district. Robert Kingham, Robert Wapshott, and Thomas Dell, passing through Maidenhead to visit their brethren who were lying in Reading jail, could not refuse the opportunity of " speaking a few Words by way of Exhortation to the People," and found themselves committed accordingly at the next Quarter Sessions of 1660-1.

" Sufferings of the people called Quakers." i p. 12.

Story, in his " Journal " under date " 3rd of 10th month " 1722, tells of better success. " I had a meeting appointed at the house of John Fellows at Maidenhead. The House was small, and Notice only given to a few : But when the

Story's Journal. p. 646.

Meeting was set and my voice heard the Place was quickly crowded, and many in the Street who could not get in; and some Military Officers and Soldiers were there : and as the Lord was pleased to open in me several Gospel Truths for their Sakes, I found a very ready Passage for them among them, so that I concluded that some Good was done to them also. That night I lodged in the same House."

He also records under 22nd of 9th month, Story's Journal. p. 697. 1733, a visit to a member of the Penn family living at "Fein, about 2 miles from Maidenhead," and a meeting in the town on the next day, "small, but open and well."

On 5th September, 1777, indentures of apprenticeship were signed which bound Thomas Pole apprentice to Joseph Rickman of Maidenhead, a relation which resulted in a devoted friendship between two loyal adherents of the Society. An account of Pole is given in the Journal Supplement No. 7 of the Friends' Historical Society. Rickman was a Surgeon and Apothecary, and is believed to have lived in a small house occupying the site of 47, High Street, next to Lloyd's Bank. Rickman's son, born at Maidenhead, though designed by his father for physic, preferred architecture, and achieved considerable distinction therein. His book, "An Attempt to Discriminate the Styles of Architecture in England, from the Conquest to the Reformation," was long a standard work, while his churches and other buildings were both numerous and important. Of the friendship existing between the elder Rickman and Pole the

latter writes, " Our hearts are knit together as
the hearts of David and Jonathan." On his
marriage Pole spent a day or two with his friend
at Maidenhead, and, when illness prostrated
him, Rickman did not hesitate to take the long,
and in those days, tedious and expensive journey
to Cirencester to see him, though the duration
of the visit could only be measured by hours.
Beyond the above, and Elwood's adventure as
recounted elsewhere, Quaker literature has little
to say of Maidenhead.

In 1801 the Friends were sufficiently numerous
to build a Meeting House. This was erected in
West Street, then known as the Back Lane.
Mr. John Cooper's estimate for the erection of
this Meeting House is preserved in the Maidenhead Museum. It is dated 31 Jan., 1801, and
the price quoted is £224 2s. od. An entry in
Maid. R. 194. the Municipal Books of 7th October, 1803,
directs " that the certificate of Hannah Wilson
and Rachel Newbury that a building in Back
Lane is to be used for worship by protestant
dissenters be filed among the records." The
edifice and the Society are connected with the
Reading Quarterly Meeting, but the present
number of Friends is very small.

WESLEYAN METHODIST.

Wesleyan Methodism was introduced into
Maidenhead in 1829 by Mr. John Higgs, a
Maidenhead tradesman, whose upbringing had
been anything but " methodistical," but who

had been induced to attend a Methodist service at Windsor, which effectually changed the whole course of his life. His successful request to the Mayor for the use of the Town Hall for a sermon brought a perfect hornet's nest about the ears of that dignitary, for with the exception of an occasional meeting in aid of the Bible Society, little in the shape of religion, to say nothing of Methodism, had ever intruded into that structure. The service was, however, held on 2nd July, 1829, and a Methodist Church formed, which found a home, first at Post Office Lane (the road on the South of High Street next to No. 27), and then in Bridge Street, where a chapel was erected, many times enlarged, and finally vacated in 1858 for the present building, at the top of High Street, which was then purchased from the Countess of Huntingdon's Connexion, and which in its turn has again and again been enlarged and improved. A Sunday School, erected by the side of the Bridge Street Chapel, was removed to High Street, and subsequently removed again to make way for the present extensive block of School buildings. On each occasion the foundation stone was laid, or re-laid, by Mr. Robert Walker, the writer's father, and bears the three dates of 7th June, 1855, 9th November, 1858, and 21st May, 1877. The Entrance Porch and Choir Vestry date from 1929, and are part of a series of extensions and improvements undertaken to celebrate the Centenary of Methodism in Maidenhead.

Prior to 1898 the clock outside the building was the one which formerly did duty at Bray

Church. The Bell in the turret is believed to have come also from Bray. It bears the inscription SAMVELL KNIGHT MADE MEE 1703.

PRIMITIVE METHODIST.

This denomination has been represented in Maidenhead from 1845. It began by occupying that room over the granary in Market Street which has been the birthplace or nursery of more than one religious and philanthropic society. Later a room was occupied in Post Office Lane, as it was then called, behind 27 High Street, but the meetings were only occasional, and it was not till 1858 that regular services were instituted, first in a room in Albert Street, then in Bridge Street, and in 1859 in the Bridge Street Chapel recently vacated by the Wesleyans. The removal to Queen Street took place in 1882, when a new chapel was erected there at a cost of £1,511, and with a seating capacity of 230.

ROMAN CATHOLIC.

Modern Roman Catholicism in Maidenhead is indirectly a product of that ecclesiastical controversy with which the name of a former curate of Maidenhead, the Rev. G. C. Gorham, is inseparably associated, and which has been referred to in another chapter. The legal decisions in this case, declaring explicitly that the Church of England was not bound to the doctrine of baptismal regeneration, and, by Hutton's Life of Manning. pp. 55 & 71. implication, that Civil Courts had jurisdiction in doctrinal and spiritual matters, were the determining factors that led not a few to exchange the Anglican for the Roman Communion. Amongst these was William, eldest son of William Wilberforce, the philanthropist and leader in the anti-slavery movement. Mr. Wilberforce came to reside in Maidenhead in 1867, making his home at Ives Place (which he re-named Saint Ives) and opening his house for Roman Catholic services, the first of which was held in his study in August of that year. At the entrance gates of the Ives Place estate stood the old " Bull " Inn. This was utilised as a priest house, a part of it being adapted for divine service, until a school chapel was built and opened at the corner of Bridge Street and Foreleaze Lane in 1871. The present Church of St. Joseph in the Cookham Road was erected at a cost of £3,000, and opened for worship on 18th December, 1884. The completed design for this church includes chancel, transepts, and a handsome central square tower, but so far only the nave has been built. The Schools adjacent to the church were erected in 1892.

OTHER DENOMINATIONS.

There has been no Presbyterian Church in Maidenhead for many years. In the manuscript " List of Dissenting Congregations in different Brit. Mus. Counties," prepared by the Rev. Josiah Thompson of Clapham, it is stated that in 1715 there was at Maidenhead a Presbyterian congregation of about one hundred. In 1772 it is stated to have been " small." It is to be noted also that the Rev. William Brice, who was ejected from Henley in 1662, and who came to reside at Monkendons, Maidenhead, which belonged to his family, is described as a " presbyterian " in a License to hold services in his own house at Maidenhead, dated 25th July, 1672, and issued under the short-lived Declaration of Indulgence of Charles II.

Cal. St.
Pap. Dom.

The Salvation Army came to Maidenhead in 1885, establishing themselves in Bridge Street in the premises until then used by the Primitive Methodists, and afterwards in a new "Barracks" in Fordeage Road. Their first service was conducted by Captain Smith, a female officer, on 6th February, 1885.

Several companies of Plymouth Brethren have at various times held services and conducted successful Sunday School work in halls or private houses, but up to now no permanent structure has been erected by them.

The Christadelphians and the Catholic Apostolic Church have occasionally put themselves in evidence, but they have never organised any community in the town.

The Christian Scientists and the Theosophical Society have also established themselves.

CHAPTER XIV.

SCHOOLS.

MAIDENHEAD boasts no "ancient seat of learning." Yet people must have learned somehow, and it is more than probable that in past times the Chaplain, or Incumbent, of St. Mary's was the chief instructor in things secular as in things sacred. The chaplaincy of the Rev. John Dawson in the reign of Charles I. has already been referred to, and mention made of his differences with the Corporation. Part of these touched his remuneration for teaching, and in the end the town undertook to pay him " 4d. weekly for every scholar learning English only, and 6d. for such as learned to write or cypher, instead of 3d. and 4d. as formerly."

Cal. St. Pap. Dom. 23rd June, 1634.

The School at Bray, founded about 1682 by William Cherry, the squire of Shottesbrook, doubtless numbered many Maidenhead boys amongst its scholars, and from time to time pious donors left bequests of a more or less educational character, but what arrangements were made to carry out their wishes will probably never be known. An entry in the Corporation records for 25th March, 1743, shows that at that date and for some time previously the town appointed a Schoolmaster; Mr. Geo. Hobbs being then chosen in place of Mr. Wm. Cave, deceased, and his remuneration was to be "the £5 a year given

Maid. R. 190.

by Mrs. Merry as also £4 a year given by Mr. Abraham Spoor." As the demand increased it was chiefly met by private enterprise, and there is no record of any public attempt to meet educational requirements until the foundation of the NATIONAL SCHOOLS in 1817. The matter had been talked of for some months, and in the April of that year the Corporation gave it to be understood that on such a school being started they would endow it with the charitable education funds at their disposal. This, how-ever, they subsequently found they had no legal power to do. The first general meeting of the promoters was held at the Sun Inn on 22nd September, 1817, when it was resolved, amongst other things, to apply to the Prince Regent for a donation. A few weeks later, on 6th October, 1817, a Society was formally constituted under the title of " The Maidenhead National School Society for the education of the Poor in the principles of the Established Church." The Scholars were to be taught the liturgy and catechism, and to attend the Sunday services of the English Church, and no religious tract was to be used in the School unless published by the Society for Promoting Christian Knowledge. The Rev. C. Goddard, Archdeacon of Lincoln, was the first Honorary Secretary, and Mr. Robert Harris the first Treasurer.

At first it was proposed to erect two schools, one at Bray and one in Maidenhead, but the proposition fell through, as did an attempt to set up a joint school at Bray.

At last a site was procured on the north of

Minutes of
Md. Nat. Sch.

" the Henley Road " (now St. Mark's Road),
and a disused gravel pit with some adjacent land,
described in the original deed as lying "opposite
to the Fleece Inn " (now the Windsor Castle)
and "near the Folly," was conveyed to the High
Steward and Chaplain and their successors as
trustees. Mr. Edward Barlow's tender of £420,
subsequently increased by £10, was accepted,
and the schools were opened on Friday, 26th
March, 1819. The total cost, including school,
schoolmaster's house, site, law costs, &c., but
not including furniture and fittings, was
£556 12s. od. The first Master and Mistress
were Mr. and Mrs. John Lane, who produced
" certificates from the Central School, Baldwin
Gardens, that they had gone through the proper
course of instruction of the National Society
education." The salary was to be £50 for the
Master and £25 (shortly after increased to £30)
for the Mistress, who was also to have half the
profit from the sewing done by the girls. Fifty
faggots and 3½ chaldrons of coal were allowed
for the house and school, but £5 was to be
deducted from the Master's salary as an
equivalent for the house and garden. The
curriculum comprised, in addition to the religious
instruction, reading, writing, and arithmetic;
with knitting, making up and mending clothes,
and household work for the girls. A committee
of ladies " assisted " the mistress in the girls'
department, supervising the instruction, and
calling into the committee-room and examining
from time to time such classes as they thought
proper. Two managers attended every week to

admit new scholars, and the duties of School Attendance Officer were discharged by visitors who mapped out the town between them. So successful was the School that within three weeks it was overcrowded, and additional accommodation had to be provided for another 50 scholars.

At one time a School Magazine seems to have been in existence, as it was reported on 12th May, 1824, that nineteen boys and fourteen girls wished to take it in. They were to pay a halfpenny a fortnight and the School funds made up the balance. The Corporation made annual grants from Spoor's and Merry's Charities, and acquired the right to nominate a certain number of pupils. These were admitted on examination, and in 1826 the subjects of examinations were, the Church Catechism, Reading the Sermon on the Mount, and questions on the 1st Chapter of Scripture History. The scholars were annually entertained in the school room in the summer at a School Feast of boiled beef and plum pudding, when various rewards were also distributed. In 1828 a clothing club was started, 8d. being added to every 4s. 4d. contributed by the scholars. Bye-Rules, formulated somewhat later, relaxed the requirements of attendance at St. Mary's in cases where parents desired their children to attend elsewhere, but provided that "The children must be clean and neat—with their hair cut short; orderly in the streets; attentive at School; well-behaved at Church; and respectful to their Superiors," the last requirement probably being not the least.

Some of the foregoing details are trivial and

domestic, but in view of the great advance made in education during the past few years no apology is offered for presenting this picture of an elementary day school of more than one hundred years ago.

In. 1863 the land at the Folly was exchanged for a site called Oxen Close in East Street, where the new and spacious buildings were erected which have been the home of the National School ever since.

The BRITISH SCHOOL was the next to appear, under the title of " The Maidenhead British School for Boys." It was established about 1848—its first Report is for the year ending 31st December, 1848—and owes its origin almost entirely to the enterprise of the Congregationalists. Their Pastor, the Rev. T. Davis, was one of the Secretaries, and almost every one of the Committee was a member of the Congregational Church. It was assisted at the start by an outfit grant from the British and Foreign School Society, and in its first year recorded an average attendance of between 60 and 70. It was subsequently made a mixed school, ran a very successful educational career, and was finally handed over to the Local Education Authority to become a Municipal School in 1903.

The WESLEYAN DAY School was commenced in 1863, and it too, after many years of useful and honourable service, became a Municipal School in 1907.

The elementary schools in connexion with ALL SAINTS' parish were opened in 1857.

They have been repeatedly enlarged and extended, and at the present time may fairly challenge comparison with any kindred establishment for miles round.

The ROMAN CATHOLIC Schools were commenced in Bridge Street in 1871, and were removed to the present buildings adjoining the Church in Cookham Road in 1892.

GORDON ROAD elementary schools are Maidenhead's response to the demands of the Education Act of 1902. Designed by Mr. E. J. Shrewsbury in accordance with the latest ideas on educational buildings, and fitted with every modern appliance, they bid fair to carry on with greater fulness the work of the two schools, British and Wesleyan, which they supersede. The Foundation Stone was laid by the present writer in the year of his mayoralty on 12th July, 1906, and the schools were opened in the following April.

Of " Academies for Young Gentlemen," and " Seminaries for Young Ladies," there were several in the early years of the 19th century. One in Market Street, kept by a Mr. Phillips, occupied the building which had been a Congregational Chapel, and subsequently became the "Hope" public-house. Mr. Such's "Academy" in Bridge Street was quite an institution in its day, and flourished for a lengthened period. Here for many years were educated the Scholars who derived their education from Spoor's Charity. Miss Appleton's " Establishment for Young Ladies " at Northwick Terrace also deserves mention. It was a superior "finishing" school.

Another school, which had a long run of public favour, was that founded about 1820 by Miss Kekwick, a Quaker lady One of her pupils, Alderman Mackie (d. 1908), used to say that Miss Kekwick "gave a holiday every Thursday, that she might go to 'Meeting,' and spent all Wednesday afternoon trimming her cap." The school was first held in a small house on the North side of the private road leading from King Street to Messrs. Nicholsons' brewery, but afterwards in a house in South Street, now pulled down to make way for the County Police Officers' Apartments. Here quite a number of well-known Maidenhead residents, both ladies and gentlemen, received their early training. Miss Kekwick, though no longer young, eventually married, and gave up her school. One of her former pupils remembers, as a girl, being many times sent into the garden to gather violets to be enclosed in letters to the favoured gentleman. But the days of Mavor's and Carpenter's Spelling Books, of Magnall's Questions, and Pinnock's History and Geography and Grammar have long since passed away, and these schools—let no one scorn them, for they did good work in their day—have given way to the larger buildings, more liberal equipment, and scientific methods of such modern private schools as Craufurd College, Maidenhead College, Cordwalles, Castle Hill Collegiate, and Craufurd House.

The needs of public secondary education have

been met by the establishment of Secondary
Schools for both boys and girls. The former was
started in 1894 by a limited liability company
under the name of "THE MAIDENHEAD
MODERN SCHOOL." It met for some months
in the Cliveden Hall, Queen Street, while its
new buildings in High Town Road were being
erected. It was, however, found impossible to
keep pace with those Government requirements
which were the conditions of securing Government grants, and the School was handed over to
the Berks County Authority, who carry it on in
their premises in Shoppenhanger's Road.

The GIRLS" SCHOOL was started by the
Berks Education Authority in 1905. For a
time it found a home in the Technical Institute,
but was subsequently transferred to more convenient premises known as "The Elms," on
Castle Hill.

The TECHNICAL INSTITUTE started life
in 1881 as an Art Class, meeting in Brock Lane
School, and then for a brief period in a room
over a warehouse in Queen Street. But the
excellent character of the teaching triumphed
over all deficiencies of environment, and in due
time the Art Class became an Art School, and
sought a home more worthy of its achievements,
and offering more scope for its future development. This was found in 1896, when the
Trustees of Kidwell's Park placed at the disposal
of the Corporation an excellent site in Marlow
Road, and the Town Council, at an outlay of
£6,250, erected, fitted and furnished the present
handsome building from the designs of Mr. E. J.

Shrewsbury. To the study of Art there was in due course added that of Science, Literature, and Commercial subjects, and the future is doubtless destined to see many further expansions of, and additions to its usefulness.

CHAPTER XV.

SPORT.

ARCHERY.

FEW of our sports are more ancient than Archery, and in former times none were more important. Down to the reign of Henry VIII. all that the rifle is now the bow was then. On skill in the use of the bow depended largely a nation's place amongst other nations, and that England bore herself so bravely on many a battlefield is due not a little to her expert bowmen. Henry VIII. did much to encourage Archery at a time when it was beginning to decline. It was then that the entry appears in the Cookham Court Rolls that " the tithing man presents that there are no archery butts, and the inhabitants are ordered to provide them under a penalty." Butts had been set up all over the country, and the names linger to this day in St. Mary's Butts, Reading; The Butts' Close, Hitchin; Newington Butts; and Butts' Piece, Cookham. For their practice, Maidenhead men repaired to the Old Field, which, prior to the enclosure, stretched from Bray to the Bath Road at Maidenhead, and carried rights of common pasture which had existed at least as far back as 1340, when an enquiry was held by royal command concerning these said common rights, which was attended by men bearing such local names as Thomas de

Foxle, John de Shobenhangre, Robert de Shyplake, and Benedict de Dillone. In this Old Field many an archery match took place, and one of these is commemorated in the well-known, but not always correctly quoted, inscription on a brass plate fixed to the South wall of the chancel of Clewer Church.

> " He that liethe vnder this stone
> Shott with a hvndred men him selfe alone
> This is trew that I doe saye
> The matche was shott in ovlde felde at Bray
> I will tell yov before yov go hence
> That his name was Martine Expence."

RACING.

Maidenhead Races were at one time quite an important function, were patronised by royalty, and regularly supported by the Corporation. Entries appear in the Bridgemasters' Accounts of a five guineas subscription paid from time to time. Such an entry appears on 25th October, 1770. The " Racing Calendar," which was first published in 1773, contains records of the Maidenhead fixture for that and every subsequent year down to 1787. It lasted three days, usually at the end of September, and three chief events are annually calendared, though one of them, the Town Plate of £50 for 4 year olds, sometimes fell through " for want of horses." The races were run in heats, some of four and some of two miles. On the 27th September, 1787, George III. and the whole of the Royal Family were present, Lord Donegal and Messrs. Godfrey Smith and Spencer taking prominent

Maid. I. 66, p. 16.

Powys, p. 229. V. C. H.

part as Stewards about that time. After 1787 there is no further record for some years, but mention is made in 1801 of a £5 subscription race at Maidenhead on September 28th of that year for a silver cup, value £50, and the remainder in specie, when Mr. Spencer's bay mare, Luisa, beat Mr. Smith's chestnut filly.

Silver.

The Course was on the South side of Altwood Road and the Bath Road, occupying a large extent of common land stretching from Tittle Row to Cox Green, and from Boyne Hill to Canon Chalk Pit. The whole of this land was then open and joined on to Maidenhead Thicket.

Silver.

Another recognised track extended from Camley Corner in a southerly direction to a point in the lane leading to the Thatched Cottage and Waltham Siding. Mr. Silver remembers seeing a race there when Mr. John Higgs, at that time the owner of a very fine animal, beat Mr. Tagg, the landlord of the Sun Inn. The races were discontinued about 1815.

BOATING.

Situated as Maidenhead is on the loveliest reach of the Thames, it would be a strange thing if boating had not formed a prominent item in local sport and recreation. While this is so to-day, it is remarkable that it is only of comparatively recent years that it has taken front rank in such matters. The late Mr. Henry Cooper has stated that one boat comprised the entire fleet at Maidenhead when George IV.

became King in 1820. Outriggers were things
of the future, and such elegant and well appointed
craft as we now see by the score for rowing,
punting or paddling, contrast strangely with
the few heavy lumbering tubs that then met the
eye. Yet there were those who felt the attraction Sporting
Mag., 1822.
of the river, even in those days, and a memorable
aquatic feat was performed on Thursday, 15th
August, 1822, when for a considerable wager
Viscount Newry and five of his servants, men
not accustomed to the work, rowed from Oxford
to London in eighteen hours. Precisely as Great
Tom struck the hour of three in the morning,
the boat left Oxford, and at 8h. 58m. 30s. p.m.
arrived at Godfrey and Searle's wharf, Westminster Bridge, winning the bet with just one
minute and a half to spare. When we consider
the locks that had to be negotiated, and the
character of the vessel in which the journey was
made, we shall scarcely find fault with the
opinion of the day " that an instance of greater
skill and prowess is scarcely to be found on
record." The strain was immense, and one of
the crew never entirely recovered from it. They
were all Maidenhead or Cookham men, and their Silver.
names were,

Viscount Newry	William Wigg
Thomas Lamb	William Lamb
Henry Spratley	Thomas Wigg

In modern times boating has been organised
by the formation of a Rowing Club which dates
from 12th July, 1876, when at a meeting in the
Town Hall under the presidency of Mr. R.
Hall-Say, a Club was formed which with vary-

ing fortunes has continued to the present. Regattas have been instituted, and on the Maidenhead Course in Bray Reach, as on other waters, the Club has had its share of success. It won the Marlow Town Cup, which was given by Mr. T. O. Wethered, M.P., in 1870, in 1879, 1907, 1908, and 1909. The Henley Town Cup, a beautiful piece of plate dating from 1837, it won in 1902, 1903, 1907, and 1908, and the Orkney Cottage Challenge Cup has also been amongst its trophies, whilst in 1924 it won the Thames Challenge Cup at Henley.

In the early years of the Club Mr. W. E. Beal was the Honorary Secretary, his services in that capacity being recognised in 1880 by the presentation of a gold watch suitably inscribed.

FISHING.

Fishing has for centuries taken prominent place amongst Maidenhead Sport. The original deed of Henry VI. authorising the foundation of the Maidenhead Guild grants " all the River under the same Bridge and extending itself along fifty feet on the South side of that Bridge, and fifty feet on the North side of the same Bridge on both banks together with the Ground Bed and Fishery of the same and other its appurtenances." Leases of this fishery were granted by the Corporation in 1584 to Edwarde Alcleyn, and to John Cherry in 1681. About 1873 the " Maidenhead, Cookham and Bray Thames Angling Association " was formed to

Maid. J. 79.

Maid. J. 84.

improve and preserve the fishing from the Shrubbery to Monkey Island, this being the unpreserved water between the limits of the Marlow and Windsor Associations. Mr. Charles Bradlaugh, M.P., was for some years a member, and if he had astonished a good many people both in theological and political circles, such performances were far outdone when he scandalised the Association by landing a trout under the prescribed size. But as the honourable gentleman hastened to apologize, nothing more was said, and he continued a welcome member till his death. The Association had a good exhibit at the International Fisheries Exhibition in 1883, and was awarded a silver medal and a Diploma of Honour.

SWIMMING.

A good many attempts have been made to provide facilities for swimming in the river. At one time a bathing stage existed at the backwater by the side of the Gas Works. Various points on the banks have been recognised as "bathing places," and more recently the water near the bridge has been used by reason of its vicinity to the premises of the Rowing Club. None of these arrangements have been really satisfactory. The impossibility of providing dressing boxes on the banks, the presence of weeds in the water, and the distance of all these places from the Town have all been serious drawbacks, and were not effectually met till

Mr. William Hamblett opened a large bath, 120 ft. long by 40 ft. wide, and holding 170,000 gallons, by the side of Hamblettonian Hall (now a motor-garage) which he had just erected in Market Street. The opening ceremony was performed on 12th August, 1876, by the Mayor, Mr. E. W. Mackie, with the help of a glass of champagne, which he threw into the water.

The opening of this bath was followed by the establishment of a Swimming Club, which continued for some years. Races, water-festivals and water-polo matches were organised, and a branch formed of the National Life-Saving Society. The closing of the bath caused an unfortunate break in these institutions, but the establishment by the Corporation of a large and well-appointed open-air bath gave them all a new lease of life. The new structure, which was opened on 24th June, 1909, by the Mayor, Mr. D. Bidmead, is 100 feet long and 40 feet wide, and holds 117,000 gallons of water. Swimming is now cultivated by the elementary day schools, and a handsome challenge shield presented in 1907 by Mr. Curtis has done much to encourage this useful and health-giving sport. The first contest for Mr. Curtis' shield, on 19th September, 1907, resulted in a tie between two teams of four each, representing respectively the Modern Secondary School and Boyne Hill Church of England Elementary School.

Long distance swimming has been encouraged by the gift by Mr. E. Dunkels of a Challenge Cup, open to resident members of the Swimming Club, the course being from Cookham Ferry to

Boulter's Weir. On the occasion of the first contest on 26th August, 1909, Mr. A. G. Griffiths, the winner, covered the distance in 38 minutes.

HUNTING.

The Royal Buckhounds hunted this and the surrounding district for some seven hundred years. At first an official pack, then the private pack of the Sovereign, and later an official institution whose Master was a State Official, it followed the wild deer for centuries. Then, as one puts it, came "civilisation in the shape of the deer-cart," until the neighbourhood becoming increasingly unsuitable for the sport, the royal pack was discontinued in 1901.

For many years the Easter Monday fixture was at the "Coach and Horses" on Maidenhead Thicket, where a large field used to assemble under the Master of the Buckhounds, and that prince of huntsmen, Charles Davis. The "Bear" Hotel and the old Wycombe Branch Station on Castle Hill were also favourite meeting places.

The Garth Hunt is the successor of a pack founded in 1816, and known as the Bramshill Hunt, but the district it hunted was too unwieldy and was eventually divided. The Eastern division fell to Mr. Garth, who held his opening meet on 8th November, 1852, and retained his Mastership till his resignation in 1902. He has been succeeded in his office by

Mr. R. H. Gosling, Major Jackson, Lord Dorchester and Capt. H. S. Chinnock (joint) and Col. F. C. Barker.

The late Prince Consort kept a pack of harriers and hunted them for some years, when he passed them on to H.R.H. the Prince of Wales (King Edward), who handed them over to the Farmers of Berks and Bucks under the Mastership of Sir Robert Harvey, Bart. Mr. W. H. Grenfell (Lord Desborough) was for some time Master of this pack. Mr. Phipps followed Mr. Grenfell, and was followed by Cap. Cotton, and Mr. P. G. Barthropp, who held the Mastership till, on the discontinuance of the Royal Buckhounds, the pack was converted into the Berks and Bucks Farmers' Staghounds, when they were taken over by Sir Robert Wilmot, Bart. Sir Robert retired in 1906, and was succeeded by Messrs. F. W. and A. H. Headington as joint Masters, with kennels and deer paddocks at "Highway," Maidenhead. The present Master (1931) is Major E. W. Shackle, and the kennels are at Cookham Dean.

Each of these packs could tell its tale of adventure and wonderful runs. In 1841 the Royal Buckhounds ran a deer to Euston Station, and somewhere in the 70's they ran a deer to Marston Gate beyond Aylesbury. The Berks and Bucks Farmers' Staghounds, too, preserve the memory of a run from Maidenhead to Strathfieldsaye after an animal known as the "bald faced hind."

V. C. H.

CRICKET.

To Maidenhead belongs the honour of the first
record of cricket in Berkshire. In the *Daily
Chronicle* of 22nd June, 1793, appeared the
following advertisement :—

CRICKET.

A grand match will be played next Monday [June 24] in Lord's
Cricket Ground, Marybone, between nine Gentlemen of the
Marybone Club and two of Middlesex against eleven of the
Maidenhead Club for 500 guineas a side. The wickets to be
pitched at eleven o'clock and the match played out.

PLAYERS.

Marybone Club. Earl Winchelsea, Capt. Cumberland, S.
Louch, Esq., R. Wyatt, Esq., — Newnham, Esq., — Nicoll,
Esq., G. Dehaney, Esq., — Tufton, Esq., H. Fitzroy, Esq.,
Bedster, Lord.

Maidenhead. G. East, Esq., — Quarm, Esq., W. Sale, Monk,
Gill, Shackell, Carter, Thompson, Finch, Ray, Lawrence.
Admission 6. An ordinary at Two o'clock.

The result was a win for Maidenhead.

Maidenhead   1st 140 2nd 185
M. C. C.   1st 75 2nd 131

A return match was played on 25th and 26th
July, when Maidenhead again won by 85 runs,
scoring 37 and 191 to the M. C. C.'s 73 and 70.
The T. Lord who played in these matches was
the owner of Lord's Cricket Ground, London,
which still bears his name.

The *Sporting Magazine* for 1794 records
another match. " Last month a grand match of
cricket was played at Old Field, near Maidenhead, between two select elevens of England for
1,000 guineas. This match was made between
R. Leigh and E. Morant, Esqres. Result in
favour of Old Field Club, 89 runs." It is said

that on one of the occasions of a match in the Old Field the Londoners were so disgusted at hearing the Bells of Bray Church proclaiming the victory of their adversaries that they turned their backs on an excellent luncheon and retired in high dudgeon.

The modern Maidenhead Cricket Club dates from 1849, and its records dating from 1850 are carefully preserved. It is probable that very few Clubs can show such a series of score sheets. The back-bone of the Club was undoubtedly the Leigh family, one of which, Mr. Edward E. Austen-Leigh, in a match at Maidenhead between the Gentlemen of Berks and the Gentlemen of Sussex scored 161 not out.

An interesting match was played in Kidwell's Park on 1st and 2nd July, 1853, between Dean and Wisden's United All England Eleven and a Maidenhead Eighteen. The Eighteen won by 11 runs. Maidenhead 100 and 79, All England 59 and 109. The ground being somewhat limited, men were posted in an adjoining field to mark down the ball, but their services were very little required. The Maidenhead fielding is said to have been excellent, and, according to the *Field,* brought "great credit to the club." Mr. William Nicholson (d. 1916), once amongst the foremost of local cricketers, was one of the heroes of this match, as was also Mr. Justice Chitty.

On 21st July, 1894, a Century match was played between Maidenhead and M. C. C. in the ground of Orkney College, Maidenhead. Such an event is rare, if indeed it is not unique in the history of Cricket. The game was not a very

brilliant one, and was decided on the first
innings in favour of the visitors. M. C. C. 77
and 97, Maidenhead 51. Maidenhead was
represented by F. M. S. Parker, H. Bacon,
F. C. B. Welch (Capt.), A. G. Robertson,
H. Manley, F. D. Browne, H. Parker, R.
Nicholson and H. Edwards—all local men—
assisted by two Surrey professionals, Brockwell
and Watts. The M. C. C. team comprised B. F.
Grieve, Whitehead, M. H. Routledge, J. H.
Farmer, W. H. Mann, A. Bird (Capt.), S. S.
Green, J. S. Muggeridge, Butt, C. B. Palmer,
Richardson.

" Municipal Cricket " has occasionally been
indulged in, when the Corporation and their
officials have contended with varying success
against similar teams from neighbouring towns.
Alderman Nicholson, though past 80 years of
age, played in 1903 against both Wycombe and
Henley, and not only played but scored.

FOOTBALL.

The Maidenhead Football Club was founded
in 1870 under Association Rules, with green and
black as its colours, subsequently changed to red
and black. Its first president was Mr. J. H.
Clark, who achieved considerable distinction in
his day as an umpire, officiating in that capacity
in 1874 in the Association Final at Lillie Bridge.
When the Club was first started fifteen a side
was the order of the day. The first match, in
which the writer took part, was in response to a

challenge from Windsor, and came off in Bond's Meadow, now covered with houses, on the East side of Maidenhead Bridge and South of the high road. The tactics of Maidenhead were simplicity itself. Whenever a Windsor man had the ball two Maidenhead men were to rush at him; one was to knock him down, and the other take on the ball. The result was a draw, to the amazement of everybody, and certainly not least to the Windsor team. For some years Maidenhead was conspicuously successful. In 1871-2 it played 17 matches, losing only one—that against the Crystal Palace in the second round for the Association Cup. Latterly, as other places became more expert and stronger competitors came into the field, honours have been more divided.

The Maidenhead Norfolkians' Football Club was founded in 1884, and after a very successful career, carrying off its full share of trophies in the various local and other competitions for which it entered, was in 1919 amalgamated with the Maidenhead Club, which has since been known as The Maidenhead United Football Club.

GOLF.

The "royal game," which has come so much into vogue of late years, has duly established itself at Maidenhead also. The Golf Course is one of 18 holes, and it situated on the Shoppenhangers Road. The membership of the Club is limited to two hundred and fifty.

CYCLING.

The honour of being the first man to ride a bicycle in Maidenhead is claimed by, and usually accorded to, Mr. H. J. Timberlake, whose Cycle Works, established here about the end of the 60's, rapidly acquired considerably more than a local reputation. The following is an interesting paragraph from the first issue of the *Maidenhead Advertiser*, dated July 28th, 1869 :

PEDESTRIANISM *versus* BICYCLFISM.—The first contest in this neighbourhood between a pedestrian and bicyclist, took place on Friday evening last, upon the Reading Road, Maidenhead Thicket, and an immense number of people, including many of the neighbouring gentry, assembled to witness the event. The contest was between Mr. Louis Rumball, the winner of the mile-and-half champion Steeple Chase Cup, at Chertsey, and of several other races, and Mr. H. J. Timberlake, the velocipedist, for £10 a side, and a chaste silver tankard, which was supplied by Mr. Hobson, of Houndsditch. The race-course was a mile in length, the starting-point being the Thicket Tollgate, and the goal being a little beyond " Bath Cottage." The race commenced at twenty-three minutes to eight o'clock. When about thirty yards from the toll-gate the bicyclist " came to grief," falling upon his right side and sustaining severe bruises. The pedestrian, who was also bruised by the accident, won the race without further opposition. The mile was run in four minutes and fifty-seven seconds. Mr. Montgomery (surgeon) was luckily upon the spot and immediately attended to the bicyclist. The upset was occasioned by some mounted gipsies and a butcher's cart being upon the race-course. The prize-tankard was presented to the fortunate winner by Mr. Stubbs. A collection was then made in aid of an Amateur Athletic Club, which is being formed. Mr. Rumball has accepted another challenge from Mr. Timberlake for double the value of the tankard, and £20 a side.

The Maidenhead Wanderers Bicycle Club has for a number of years held a meeting in Kidwell's Park on the August Bank Holiday, which has attracted considerable entries, and shown some excellent sport.

BOWLS.

Of recent years this game has come into increased favour, and several Bowling Clubs have been started.

LAWN TENNIS.

This game also has been well represented in Maidenhead, and has called several Clubs into existence.

OTHER SPORTS.

Of Bull-baiting and Cock-fighting there is no record, nor was Maidenhead a pugilistic centre. What prize fighting was done took place at Knowl Hill or Hurley. On the occasion of the great battle between Jim Belcher and Joe Berks on 25th November, 1801, at Hurley, both combatants passed the previous night at Maidenhead, Belcher putting up at the " Sun," and Berks at the " Bear."

V. C. H.

CHAPTER XVI.

SOME MAIDENHEAD INSTITUTIONS.

THE MAIDENHEAD HOSPITAL.

THE Hospital was founded in 1879. Its architect was Mr. A. L. Cooper, and its first president was Mr. John Hibbert, of Braywick, who till his death was a most generous supporter of the institution. In 1882 a mortuary, ambulance house and other conveniences were added. On the coming of age of his son in 1900, Mr. W. Waldorf Astor, of Cliveden, signalised the event by a present of £10,000 to the hospital funds. Additional land was now acquired, a new operating room erected and fitted with every modern requirement, and several other improvements made to the establishment. A sum of £10,000, left by the late Mr. Samuel Lewis to found an extension in memory of his Wife, has been so utilised, and on 14th December, 1908, the "Ada Lewis Wing" was formally opened by H.R.H. The Princess Christian, who then for the second time honoured the hospital with her presence, and its Visitors' Book with her signature. Considerable extensions and additions have been made from time to time, including the installation of a complete X ray apparatus.

THE PUBLIC LIBRARY.

The Public Library movement in Maidenhead

dates from 9th April, 1891, when at a meeting held under the presidency of the Mayor, Mr. J. D. M. Pearce, a resolution was unanimously carried that a Free Public Library would be a benefit to the town, and should be established if the Ratepayers desired it. The Town Council were, however, of opinion that the capital outlay involved was more than the town could face, and declined to proceed, till 1902, when at the instance of the then Mayor, Councillor Good, Mr. Andrew Carnegie promised to give £5,000 to build a Free Public Library if the town would provide a site and adopt the Public Library Acts. The Acts were at once adopted, and all difficulties with regard to site were smoothed away by the generosity of Mr. William Nicholson, who, at a cost of £1,000, placed a most eligible site at the disposal of the Corporation. The opening ceremony took place on 27th October, 1904, when the High Steward, W. H. Grenfell, Esq., formally unlocked the door. The building, which is from designs by Messrs. McKewan and Cale, of Birmingham, provides for Reading and Magazine Rooms, Lending and Reference Libraries, Stores, and Librarian's House. It also gives temporary accommodation to the Town Museum.

The War Memorial.

Adjoining the Public Library stands a handsome Memorial Cross, designed by Lt.-Col. Johns, the Borough Surveyor, commemorating

the Maidenhead men who fell in the Great War
of 1914-18. Here on Armistice Day, Nov. 11th,
the Corporation and citizens have assembled
annually, and observed the "Silence." The
names of those commemorated will be found in
Appendix G.

THE RAILWAY.

The Great Western Railway can hardly be
called a Maidenhead Institution, but its coming
to the district, and the opening of its three
stations of Taplow, Maidenhead (Wycombe
Branch) and Maidenhead so greatly influenced
the fortunes of the town that it claims some
reference, however brief. Its advent is recorded
as follows in Pigot's Gazetteer, which though Pigot's
undated was evidently published about 1840. Gazetteer.
" This stupendous undertaking and rapid mode
of transit was opened as far as Maidenhead, by
an experimental trip on the 30th of May, 1838,
amidst enthusiastic expressions of delight at the
arrangements and the most lively anticipations
of its ultimate success; the distance, nearly
twenty-four miles, was accomplished somewhat
within the hour. The railway was regularly
opened for the conveyance of passengers to
Maidenhead, on the 4th June following." The
Station, afterwards known as Taplow Station,
occupied a site on land opposite the " Dumb
Bell," and nearer Maidenhead by half a mile
than the present Taplow Station. It was of the
most primitive order of architecture, and its
distance from the town was for many years a

serious inconvenience. But it was placed as near Maidenhead as the circumstances of the hour permitted, for a bridge had to be thrown across the Thames, and that could not be done in a moment. Isambard Brunel was the architect, and he resolved to outdo everyone by giving his chief arches the largest span of brickwork in the country. Each is 128 ft. in span, with a rise of 24 ft. 3 ins. The bridge is a remarkable as well as graceful structure. It was constructed in 1837-8, at a cost of £37,000, and for months after its completion tons of stone were placed on it to prevent any upward spring before it was perfectly set. It is also possessed of a wonderful echo, as every word uttered from the towing path which passes under it may be counted eight times in repetition.

The length of the bridge is 778 feet, with an original width of 30 feet, skilfully increased in 1891 to 60 feet, when the line was duplicated.

On the opening of the Wycombe Branch on 1st August, 1854, a small station was constructed where the line passes under the Bath road at Castle Hill, and did duty as Maidenhead Station till the present structure was erected in the Braywick Road, the foundation stone of which was laid on 3rd May, 1871, by the Mayor, Mr. Robert Walker.

On 1st February, 1858, the Railway Company took exception to the Borough Watch Rate, and refused to pay. They were summoned before the Borough Bench, and, though they pleaded non-liability, were ordered to pay. Then they appealed, whereupon the town took the remarkable step of dismissing the whole of the police force except the superintendent, and were favoured with a letter from the Home Secretary asking for an explanation. Finally, on taking Counsel's opinion, the Corporation found their case so uncertain that they declined to carry it further, and it is to be feared that watch-rate is still in arrear.

THE POST OFFICE.

The Post Office was originally the place, usually an inn, which supplied the horses and chaises for the conveyance of government messengers and communications, and the office of Postmaster was not always either happy or remunerative. In the "Acts of the Privy Council, 1578-1580," there is preserved a letter to Richard Lovelace, Esq., stating that Wm. Davyes has informed their Lordships that he is not able to continue to keep the post at Maidenhead. Lovelace is to assemble them of the town and see how the burden may be borne and Her Majesty served, urging " smallnes of the charge amonge so manie "; posts are not to be continued long (as it is hoped), and payment made "at Her Majesty's hands." "Their Lordships trust that they of the said town will make no difficultie in the matter." The letter is dated 26 Aug., 1579.

B.M. 2080 c.

The modern postmaster whose duty it is to receive His Majesty's mails, open them, and distribute their contents, is a much later institution. Some time in the eighteen-thirties he was found in Maidenhead installed in a room in a lane between No's 27 and 29, High Street, which became known as "Post Office Lane," the letters being taken round by a post-woman. Twenty years later one Sarney was the single postman, officiating also as Town Crier. The office has several times been removed, and at one time the postmaster was also the Town Clerk. The present buildings in High Street were erected in 1892. At the present time (1931) the staff includes 59 postmen and 58 clerks, telephonists, and others, both men and women, a total of 117. As giving some idea of the growth of Post Office business in Maidenhead, it may be mentioned that during the Christmas of 1930 (Dec. 19-25) 1,055 bags of letters were sent off, 1,020 bags were received in, and 17,663 parcels were delivered in the Maidenhead District.

THE GAS COMPANY.

Prior to 1835 Maidenhead was lit by certain oil lamps placed on brackets and standards in different parts of the town. The stout iron posts supporting the chain on the high path on the South side of Castle Hill, and bearing the name of Mr. Foster, Mayor, are the remains of these standards, the top parts having been cut off and the lower parts so utilised.

In 1833, Mr. Wm. Morley Stears, who had successfully lit with gas Stroud, Henley, and other places, issued a prospectus for the formation of a Gas Company for Maidenhead. The proposal was warmly welcomed and warmly opposed. A circular by Mr. Stears' solicitor, Mr. Samuel Naylor, is preserved, denouncing in Johnsonian periods the iniquity of the anonymous opposers, the "worthless nature" of certain "placards," and "the feeble virulence of their contents."

A Company was duly formed in 1835 with a capital of £3,000, and a Committee of Management appointed consisting of the Earl of Orkney, Rev. Walter Levett, J. E. Langton, Richard Goolden, Wm. Tagg, John Higgs, George Bennett, Charles Williams and Richard Swallow. The original deed, which is handsomely engrossed and bound, bears the signatures of a long list of shareholders, the first being that of "Charles Williams, Mayor, For the Corporation of Maidenhead, 20 shares."

The Works, which were erected on the Bucks side of the river above the bridge, have been repeatedly enlarged. The Chair of the Company has been occupied successively by Charles Williams, J. E. Langton, George Bennett, Robert Walker, E. R. Lovegrove, and J. W. Walker.

Tradition hath it that the inaugural dinner was held at the Bear Hotel, where Martha, the R. Walker. cook, spent her wedding-day in preparing it, she having that morning given her hand to Charlie, the coachman, that gentleman having previously vanquished Dick, the ostler, in fair fight in the stable yard, and so won the bride.

In 1924 the Company was amalgamated with that of Uxbridge, and became known as the

Uxbridge, Maidenhead, Wycombe and District
Gas Company.

The Waterworks Company.

The Maidenhead Waterworks Company was
incorporated by an Act of Parliament which
received Royal Assent on 28th May, 1875, with
a capital of £20,000 and borrowing powers of
£5,000; the area being the Borough of Maidenhead and the Parishes of Bray and Cookham.
The first chairman was Mr. T. J. White, who
was succeeded in February, 1877, by Mr. R.
Silver. Water was first supplied in August,
1876, when a large Swimming Bath erected in
Market Street by Mr. W. Hamblett, was filled.
There was, therefore, some point in Mr. Silver's
remark at the opening of this bath, that it was
also the opening of the local Waterworks
Company. Powers have been acquired for
increasing the capital, and also for extending
the area of supply, which now includes Hurley,
Ruscombe, White Waltham, St. Lawrence
Waltham, and Shottesbrook. The water is of
excellent quality, having been repeatedly submitted to analysis with highly gratifying results.
The sources of supply are the chalk formations
at College Avenue, Maidenhead, and at Cookham
Dean. A reservoir at Castle Hill has a capacity
of 600,000 gallons, at Cookham Dean of 500,000
gallons, at Warfield of 210,000 gallons, and at
Ashley Hill, Hurley, of 650,000 gallons.

THE ELECTRIC LIGHTING UNDERTAKING.

On the 11th October, 1897, the Town Council Corporation Minutes. decided to apply to the Board of Trade for a Provisional Order authorising the Corporation to supply electricity. The Order was granted on the 12th August, 1898.

There being some difference of opinion in the Council as to whether the Corporation should undertake the Electric Lighting or whether the powers contained in the Provisional Order should be handed over to a Private Company, it was decided to take a Poll of the Borough, which took place on the 28th April, 1899. The result was as follows :—

In favour of the Corporation		310
,,	a Private Company	118
	Majority :	192

A Committee was then appointed and commenced work at once, Messrs. Burstall & Monkhouse being retained as Consulting Engineers.

On the 1st December, 1900, the sanction of the Local Government Board was obtained to the first loan of £25,000, and since that date various other sums have been sanctioned, making the total authorised capital at the present date £45,907.

The Machinery at the Central Station was formally started by Mr. E. Gardner, M.P., on the 17th December, 1902, the current being formally switched on by Mr. W. H. Grenfell, M.P. (Lord Desborough), on the same day.

On the 15th August, 1904, the Council obtained a further Provisional Order, which, amongst other things, extended their powers of supply to parts of Taplow, Cookham and Bray, and the Corporation Mains now supply the whole of Maidenhead Court, Upper and Lower Taplow, and Bray Village.

The capacity of the undertaking when opened was 180 kilowatts. Since then transforming and converting plant has been installed, and now (1930) 2,825 K.W. can be dealt with.

The length of mains at the commencement was about five miles, which has been slowly increasing ever since, and now there are 50 miles in use.

The Chairmanship of the Electric Lighting Committee has been held successively by Councillor J. Edward Pearce, Alderman Hewitt, Councillor Good, and Alderman Stuchbery.

THE FIRE BRIGADE.

The Maidenhead Volunteer Fire Brigade was formed in 1866, and has again and again justified its existence at what but for its timely interference would have proved most disastrous fires. It has also demonstrated its skill on the review ground, frequently giving local displays as well as taking part in Metropolitan and other brigade contests. In 1893, after having been long housed in more or less unsuitable fashion, a properly equipped engine house and mess-room was provided in Park Street by the Corporation.

A magnificent and powerful steam fire-engine was supplied in 1905, and at the present time it is not too much to say that both men and appliances are worthy the one of the other.

THE PARKS.

The generosity of Mr. W. H. Grenfell, now Lord Desborough, and Mr. J. D. M. Pearce has preserved to the people of Maidenhead two open spaces, one on the north and the other on the south side of the town.

GRENFELL PARK, on the south, was placed at the disposal of the burgesses for 99 years from 29th September, 1889, at a peppercorn rent, by the gentleman whose name it bears. The lease was signed on the 21st October, 1889, on which date the Corporation and townsfolk entertained the lessor to dinner in the Town Hall.

KIDWELL'S PARK, once belonging to the family of Sir Neville Kidwell, a distinguished townsman and a former Warden, was handed over to a body of Trustees for the use of the people of Maidenhead, under a deed dated 23rd July, 1890, by Mr. J. D. M. Pearce, who for many years had taken a leading part in local affairs and had been mayor five times. The park possesses a good grass cycling track, and for many years the local Cycling Club have organised sports here on the August Bank Holiday on an extensive scale. Provision is also made for lawn tennis, football, and other games.

CLUBS.

It is impossible to enumerate all the various organisations which have existed under the general name of Clubs. Some have been of a literary and scientific character like the old " Mechanics' Institute," which after a fairly long and useful career was disbanded in the '60s. To fill the vacancy, Mr. J. D. M. Pearce started the " Maidenhead Literary Institute " in Queen Street, and this, too, but for a shorter period, served a good purpose till interest waned and the place was closed. A similar fate befel a Branch of the Young Women's Christian Association started between 1880 and 1890.

Another non-political institution which has now flourished for many years is the Working Men's Club in Norfolk Park. Founded in 1877 mainly through the instrumentality of the Rev. W. G. Sawyer, his brother, Mr. Robert Sawyer, and Mr. J. D. M. Pearce, and suitably housed, it has formed a meeting place for many besides working men. It has unquestionably met a public want, and bids fair to thrive for many years to come. The Club possesses a Library of over 1,000 volumes.

Other Clubs for the benefit of the lads and young men of the town have been frequently started by the various Churches, but the most notable attempt to cater for lads is the Boys' Club in the Cookham Road with which the name of Mr. Ernest Myer is inseparably connected. It was started in 1903. In five years 530 boys had joined, the membership in 1929 being 162.

It provides for both indoor and outdoor sports and recreation, and possesses a good Gymnasium. It has also a debating society, "first aid" lectures, and a labour bureau. The Club premises were opened by H.R.H. the Princess Christian on 14th December, 1908.

In the matter of political clubs the Conservatives have been much more successful than the Liberals. These latter have opened Clubs at various times, notably one in Broadway, and fitted them with reading and recreation rooms, but adequate support has not been forthcoming, and the rooms have been closed. Two Conservative Clubs have, however, passed out of the experimental stage. The Conservative Working Men's Club, established in 1894, is well housed in York Road in its own home, the foundation stone of which was laid on 28th February, 1901, by Captain Oliver Young, M.P. for the division. Two years later the Constitutional Club for Conservatives and Liberal Unionists was opened at 50, Queen Street, with a large and influential membership.

THE CHAMBER OF COMMERCE.

The Chamber was founded on the 4th May, 1905, at a meeting convened by the then Mayor, Councillor B. Hobbis, who was appointed its first President. Its objects were stated to be the promotion of the commercial and general interests of the town, and to assist in extending and developing its attractions for visitors and

residents. The Chamber publishes an official
" Guide to Maidenhead," and has in many ways
brought its influence to bear for the good of
the town.

The Maidenhead and District Rifle Club.

In the spring of 1906, and chiefly through the
exertions of Dr. Mason-Macfarlane, the town
was favoured with a visit from Earl Roberts,
who delivered an address on National Defence
to a large and influential gathering which
crowded the Drill Hall in Marlow Road to its
utmost capacity. The result was the founding
of the Maidenhead and District Rifle Club;
amongst the most energetic of whose members
were Capt. Bateman and Mr. B. Hobbis. The
old disused Hamblettonian Swimming Bath was
converted into a miniature range and formally
opened by the Mayor (Councillor J. W. Walker)
on 7th June, 1906. An offer of £500 from
Mr. W. W. Astor, a generous lease of land on
very advantageous terms by Lord Desborough,
and a substantial contribution from Mr. William
Nicholson enabled the Club to secure an
admirable open-air one hundred yards range at
the " Gullet " near the railway, which has been
fitted with all the latest improvements in targets
and marking gear. It was opened by Lord
Desborough on 8th May, 1907. A number of
matches have been arranged with local clubs,
and some very successful Prize Meetings
organised.

DRILL HALL.

The Drill Hall in Marlow Road is the gift to the town of Mr. J. D. M. Pearce, the donor of Kidwell's Park, who by his will left £3,000 for the building and equipping of a Drill Hall and Gymnasium. The property is vested in Trustees, and was publicly opened in 1903 during the Mayoralty of the donor's son, Councillor J. Edward Pearce. It has been largely used by the local Territorials, Athletic and Gymnastic Clubs, and others.

MUSIC AND DRAMA.

For many years the local interest in both music and the drama has found its expression in a constant succession of Societies bearing the appellations of Choral, Philharmonic, Orchestral, Operatic and Amateur Dramatic. Amongst its individual musicians Maidenhead cherishes the memory of Zerubabel Wyville, organist of St. Mary's, composer of songs and tunes that had a great run in the district, and the chief musical authority of the neighbourhood. Robert Wyville, son of the foregoing, was not only a prominent musician, but for a long time an active member of the Corporation.

Nor should we forget Mr. William Burnham, in the eighteen-fifties the recognised contra-basso for Berkshire, who with his double-bass was in constant request all over the county.

But many years before this, Maidenhead was contributing to the gaiety of nations. It is on

record that at the Feasts of the Fraternity of the
Holy Cross at Abingdon, somewhere about 1450,
" they had twelve minstrels, some from Coventry
and some from Maydenhyth, to make them
merry, to whom they gave 2/3 a-piece besides
their diet and horse-meat."

NEWSPAPERS.

Prior to 1869 the chief newspapers circulating
in Maidenhead were the *Reading Mercury,* the
Windsor Express, and the *South Bucks Free
Press.* In that year a syndicate resolved to issue
a purely local organ, and commenced the publica-
tion of the *Maidenhead Advertiser.* After a good
start it experienced some difficulties; then
Mr. F. G. Baylis, whose name will be inseparably
connected with the paper, appeared on the scene,
and a career of success was entered upon which
has been maintained to the present day. Various
competitors have from time to time arrived—and
departed. The *Maidenhead Guardian, Courier,
Times,* and *Argus* have successively appealed for
popular support, but their experience has not
been very encouraging, nor their existence very
prolonged.

THE HORTICULTURAL SOCIETY.

The Horticultural Society was founded in
1878, holding its first Show on the 29th August
of that year in the Hamblettonian Hall. The
Society, which enjoyed the patronage of their

Royal Highnesses the Prince and Princess Christian, had for its first President Mr. John Hibbert of Braywick, and for its first Chairman of Committee, Mr. Richard Silver, who sustained that office down to the year 1900.

Empire Day.

The celebration of 24th May, the birthday of Queen Victoria, as Empire Day, has now become quite one of the Institutions of the town. Inaugurated unofficially by the Mayor, Mr. B. Hobbis, in 1905, it has ever since received the recognition of the Corporation, and bids fair to become an annual function for many years to come. A prominent place in the celebration is naturally accorded to the young people of the schools, and, with a view to add interest to the proceedings, Councillor Upson in the year of his mayoralty presented a Challenge Shield for competition in flat racing by teams of four from any of the elementary schools of the town. The first race, which took place in Kidwell's Park in 1908, was won by Boyn Hill Church of England Boys' School.

CHAPTER XVII.

CHARITIES.

(i.) MUNICIPAL.

UNDER the general title of the *Municipal Charities* are comprised those founded by *Elizabeth Merry, Abraham Spoore, Mary Rixman, Thomas Ring, Margaret Poole,* and *Ralph Poole.* The first five of these were administered by the Corporation of the borough down to 1835, when, on the passing of the Municipal Corporations Act, they were transferred to a body of Trustees. Ralph Poole's Charity passed into the same hands in 1901, prior to when it had been administered privately. The whole of the Municipal Charities are now administered by a body of Trustees consisting of the Mayor (ex officio), four representative trustees appointed by the Town Council, and five co-optative trustees.

Merry's Charity. By her will dated 1st August, 1686, Mrs. Elizabeth Merry gave to the poor of Maidenhead £5 per annum, to be paid for ever out of the rents of the house wherein she lived, for putting out poor children to school. For many years the income was united with a benefaction given by Mr. Spoore, as set forth hereafter, in support of a school for boys, five boys beng maintained on this foundation. Since the provision by the nation of free elementary education the income from Merry's Charity has been applied to higher education; and, as the other charities are restricted to boys, this one is set apart for a Scholarship for girls, tenable at the County Girls' School, Maidenhead. It is to be regretted that the limited income of the Charity does not allow of more than one scholarship at a time, and even that cannot be granted every year.

Spoore's Charity. By an indenture dated 16th November, 1697, Abraham Spoore provided for the payment of £15 a year for the schooling and teaching four boys in Maidenhead, to be chosen two out of Cookham side, and two out of Bray side, to learn to read and write English, and to cast accounts, and to buy them books to learn in, and also pens, ink and paper, until they be fit to be put out as apprentice to some good handicraft trade. Provision was also made for apprenticing the boys. The funds were derived at first from a charge on the bridge tolls to which Mr. Spoore had become entitled, subsequently from property conveyed to the Corporation by Mr. John Whitfield, Mr. Spoore's trustee, by indentures of lease and release dated 20th and 21st July, 1724, the property consisting of two houses, a barn, and a lodging-house for vagrants. At the present time the property consists of a messuage in the High Street, the "Vine" public-house in Market Street, and a strip of land adjoining thereto acquired in 1902, the total income of the Charity being £137 10s. 0d. The income was at first applied, together with Merry's Charity, in the support of a school, as stated above, and in apprenticeships. Subsequently the scholars were removed to the National

School, but of recent years the Charity has been applied to scholarships‾ tenable at the County Boys' School (late Modern School), Maidenhead, and in apprenticeships, the scholarships being open to boys attending any public elementary school in the borough, and awarded in connexion with the examination for the Berks County Scholarships.

Rixman's Charity. An Indenture dated 20th July, 1628, between Geoffery White, of the one part, and Symon Winch and others, sets forth that Mary, late wife of John Lane, sometime wife and widow of John Rixman, left by will £4 10s. od. yearly to " put forth " and clothe a certain number of children dwelling in Maidenhead and in Bray parish, and to provide a dinner every third year when the corporation and churchwardens met to transact the business of the Charity. In 1772, a board of trustees was constituted, but subsequently the entire management devolved on the Corporation, and so continued till 1835. Under the powers of the Enclosure Acts, certain exchanges were effected as to parts of the property, and later on portions were sold to the Great Western Railway Company. The property now consists of a messuage at Boyne Hill, allotment ground (2a. 2r. 10p.) near the foregoing, three cottages at Boyne Hill, a close of land (5a. or. 33p.) in Maidenhead Ray, a rent for way-leave, and £234 4s. 11d. in consols. The total income is £85 18s. 6d., and is applied in apprenticeships. The provision for a dinner is not now observed.

Ring's Charity. By his will dated 20th July,

1636, Thomas Ring gave the rent and profits of his house and certain lands to the poor of the town of Maidenhead, to be distributed by the collectors of the poor. In process of time certain exchanges have taken place, and the property now consists of a piece of land (4a. 1r. 12p.) in Upper Maidenhead Field, land (3r. 21p.) at North Town, land near to with two cottages thereon, and four other cottages and gardens at North Town. On the first of these plots the lessee covenanted to expend, and has expended, not less than £1,000 in improvements. The total income of the Charity is £94. It is expended annually in flannel and coats, which are distributed to approved applicants who have made personal application to the trustees at a meeting held for the purpose, when full particulars are taken, and each case is considered on its merits.

Margaret Poole's Charity. By certain indentures dated 3rd March, 1641, Margaret Poole provided that the rents and profits of a close of land at Wargrave, Berks, known as Bare (or Beare) Innings, should be applied to the benefit of the poor of Maidenhead, in buying cloth to be given away every 1st day of November, so that two parts in three should go to those of the Cookham side of the town and the remaining third to those of Bray side. In 1801 the then trustees granted a lease of the property for a term of 500 years at a yearly rental of £30, and that sum is now the income of the Charity. It is disbursed in the same manner as Ring's Charity, and conjointly therewith.

Ralph Poole's Charity. An ancient tablet in Cookham Church states that Ralph Poole gave, by Will, £10 8s. 0d. yearly, for ever, payable out of an estate called Monkendon's. The bequest is ancient, but the date has not been ascertained. The property, which is situated in Maidenhead High Street, was prior to 1822 held by Mr. James Payn, Maidenhead's celebrated Recorder. He was in the habit of distributing bread at his house every Sunday to the value of the Charity, but after his death the distribution was for some years very irregular. Since 1901 the administration has been in the hands of the Trustees of the Municipal Charities, and is applied in sending patients to a convalescent home, providing invalid appliances, supplying books and apparatus for poor scholars, and tools for apprentices, payment of examination fees, and other non-recurrent purposes.

(ii.) Non-Municipal.

Davis' Charity. By Will dated 12th July, 1716, Mr. Charles Davis, of St. James', Westminster, left his freehold estate at Maidenhead to the overseers of Cookham and Bray in trust for the benefit of such of the poor of Maidenhead as did not receive parish alms. An annual distribution of the profits of the estate was to be made on the anniversary of the day of his death (Nov. 11th), on which occasion the incumbent of St. Mary's was to preach a sermon and receive 10s. for so doing, and the trustees were to " take to themselves 5s. a piece for a bottle of wine and a breakfast together on that day."

The property of the Charity consists of two messuages in High Street; and the present income, which was increased in 1916, is £275. The income may be applied in subscriptions or donations to hospitals and provident clubs, as well as in the provision of trade outfits for persons under 21 years of age, clothing, fuel, food or relief in sudden emergency. For some years coal tickets have been annually distributed to some 200 poor persons, and donations have been given to the various Clothing Clubs of the borough, both Anglican and Nonconformist.

The trustees are nine in number and include the Vicar of St. Mary's, the Mayor, and others.

The Samuel Lewis Old Age Pensions. Mr. Samuel Lewis, by his Will dated 12th September, 1900, left £15,000 for such charitable institutions in Maidenhead or Cookham as his trustees might select. The bequest became available in 1906, when, after paying £1,000 to the Maidenhead Working Boys' Club, and taking the decision of the High Court of Justice as to the division of the residue between Maidenhead and Cookham, Mr. Lewis' executors handed a sum of £9,000 to trustees at Maidenhead to invest and distribute the income in Old Age Pensions. The Trustees consist of the Mayor, the Vicar of St. Mary's (*ex officio*), two representative trustees appointed by the Town Council, and five co-optative trustees. The pensions are not to exceed the annual value of £30 in the case of married couples, and £20 in the case of single persons or widows, and the total income of recipients (including the present pension) may not exceed £45 for married persons, and £30 for single persons or widows. The income of the trust is available for pensions, invalid appliances, supplying books and apparatus for poor scholars, and tools for apprentices, payment of examination fees and other non-recurrent purposes.

(iii.) OTHER CHARITIES MOSTLY MORE OR LESS DENOMINATIONAL.

Whitfield's Charity. By his Will, dated 3rd October, 1728, Richard Whitfield charged certain property at Cudsdens by Wheatley, Oxon, with an annual payment of £6 10s. 0d., to be collected by whatever relation of the testator should be the occupier of the Manor House of Ives, Maidenhead, and distributed by him to six persons, housekeepers, or that have been such, in Maidenhead, who do not accept parish relief, and who frequent the Church, four of them coming from Bray side, and two from Cookham side of the town. The residue of the rent charge was to be laid out in cloth for aged men and women. The last " relation " of the Testator was Mr. Penyston Powney, who died in 1794. The property then passed by sale through several hands, each occupier always distributing the Charity as he thought well till 1837, when the Rev. G. C. Gorham, then curate of St. Mary's, remonstrated, claimed in conjunction with the Mayor the right to administer, and the Mayor and the Vicar of St. Mary's have ever since administered the Charity accordingly, one half by the Mayor, one half by the Vicar.

Seymour's Charity. Mrs. Ann Seymour, whose Will was proved 24th October, 1797, left a sum in 3 per cent. Consols sufficient to produce an annual income of £20 "to establish a school and find books and employment for poor girls residing within the corporation of Maidenhead and not being dissenters from the Church of England." Subject to a favourable report from the teacher, each girl on leaving school was to have a Bible and Prayer-book. The Will provided that the Minister of St. Mary's and representatives from the Corporation should administer this Charity, but the Corporation have long ceased to have anything to do with it. Successive Orders of the Charity Commissioners and the Board of Education have vested it in the Vicar of St. Mary's and three others. The income, formerly applied in providing clothing and books, with free education, for a certain number of girls at the National Schools, is now applied in giving clothing and a Bible and Prayer-book to girls leaving Brock Lane Sunday School, and in providing books for the general use of the Sunday School

Shapland's Charity. In 1835 Miss Charity Shapland bequeathed all her property, amounting to about £1,000, for the benefit of the poor of Maidenhead, entrusting her executor, Mr. Charles Williams, a Maidenhead surgeon, with the entire management of the bequest. By successive Orders the principal is invested in the names of the Official Trustees of Charitable Funds, and the administration of the income, amounting to £27 10s. od., is vested in the vicar and churchwardens of St. Mary's. As a general rule, clothing-tickets, value 5s. each, are distributed, one half in St. Mary's Parish, one fourth in St. Luke's, and one fourth in All Saints', and there are also grants made to St. Mary's Clothing and Maternity Clubs.

Wyvill's Charity. Mr. Robert Wyvill in 1867 left £400 to the incumbent and chapelwardens of Saint Mary's to invest the same and apply the income in the distribution of bread, coals, clothing, or otherwise, about Christmas, among the deserving poor of the Borough. The annual value of the Charity is £13 10s. 8d., and its benefits are in practice restricted to the poor of Saint Mary's, the ground of such restriction being certain directions of the testator contained in a letter dated 23rd November, 1867, and addressed to the Vicar of the Parish.

Beeney's Charity. Miss Emily Beeney, in 1883, left the residue of her estate to Miss H. M. Coney, in trust for the poor of Maidenhead. Land was at once purchased by Miss Coney, and the erection of almshouses thereon was commenced, but Miss Coney's death prevented the completion of the scheme. By an Order of the Charity Commissioners dated 15th June, 1887, the Charity was transferred to the Vicar and Churchwardens of Saint Luke's, who now distribute the income, £15 1s. 8d., in sums of 10s. each to 30 poor widows every December.

Coney's Charity. Miss Helen Mary Coney, who died in 1886, left money to the Vicars of St. Luke's and St. Mary's to provide 6s. per week to six aged couples resident in Maidenhead, and 5s. per week to certain selected widows or spinsters. The amount annually available is £141 2s. od. less income tax, and the pensioners are selected in equal proportions from the parishes of St. Luke and St. Mary.

Lady Pocock's Charities. In 1814 Dame Ann Pocock founded a Sunday School for the purpose of teaching 30 girls to read and spell, and say their catechism, and the collects for the day. She selected the girls, clothed them, and paid a schoolmistress three shillings weekly for her attendance every Sunday. On her death in 1816 Lady Pocock left a sum of money to endow the School, and also left a large number of other charitable benefactions. For some time these were in the hands of her executors, who duly administered their trusts, but by successive Orders of the Charity Commissioners these Charities are vested in Trustees and are separated into Ecclesiastical and Non-Ecclesiastical.

The former of these is in the hands of the vicars of St. Mary's, St. Luke's, and All Saints', and two other persons, and the income is £77 6s. 4d. The Sunday School was continued in rented premises till the lease expired in 1900, when the School was discontinued, the mistress receiving a pension till her death in 1908. The income is now applied for providing clothing and prizes for girls attending Church of England Schools in the Borough. The clothing is usually worth £1 per head, and the recipients are selected in equal numbers from the three ecclesiastical parishes.

The income of the non-ecclesiastical Charity is £169 7s. od., and the trustees are the same as those of the Ecclesiastical Charity, with the addition of one other selected by the Town Council, who holds office for four years, and is not necessarily a member of the Corporation.

Of the income, £50 is paid to the Vicar of St. Mary's and distributed to aged and poor recipients selected by the Vicars of the three ecclesiastical parishes.

£30 is paid to Cookham Parochial Charities.

£50 is applied in gifts of £5 to single women servants, of not less than 25 years of age, who have lived seven years in one situation in Maidenhead or its vicinity.

A weekly dole of bread was formerly given to certain poor people, and this is continued to the survivors.

From the balance a subscription is paid to the Windsor and Eton Royal Dispensary and Infirmary, about £15 is expended in Christmas gifts of food and fuel to some 75 people, and contributions are made to the three parochial coal clubs. The provisions of the Trust are not limited to these objects, but afford opportunity for dealing with a wide and varied field of exceptional necessities.

Eyle's Charity. Mr. William Micklem Eyle in 1868 bequeathed to the deacons of the Congregational Church the income from the residue of his estate, to provide for a free distribution of coals to such poor persons as the deacons might select. The bequest is now represented by a sum of money invested in Consols, and the income, amounting to £22 15s. od., is applied in distributing coal in quantities of 5, 10, or 20 cwt. to approved recipients.

(iv.) ALMSHOUSES.

Smith's Almshouses. These Almshouses, which for so many years have formed a notable feature of Bridge Street, just east of the Moor, are one of the most picturesque reminders of ancient days that the town possesses. Their long, low roof, fine old brickwork, and quaint architecture, are almost all that is now left to us of their period. Over the centre archway a tablet sets forth that " Theis Almshowses were erected and built at ye sole and proper cost and charges of Iames Smyth Esqvior Citizen and Salter of London in ye yeare of our Lord 1659." They were endowed with the income arising from various lands, the chief of which was Norden Farm, and three additional donations have since been made. One of these is an annual sum of £8 left by Mrs. Smith, the founder's widow, another is a gift, made in 1764, by Mrs. Mary Parkhurst and Miss Elizabeth Smith, two descendants of the founder, of a rent charge of £50 on land in Rotherhithe, Surrey, and the third is a bequest by Mr. George Pearce in 1878 of £1,000. A tablet in the entrance lobby of the Almshouses also sets forth that the Salters'

Company gave £100 to the re-building of St. Mary's Church in 1825, so that the alms-people might have seats there. The entire management of the Charity is in the hands of the Salters' Company, who, when there is a vacancy in the homes, receive nominations from either the Maidenhead Town Council or the Cookham Parish Council, and elect accordingly. There is accommodation for eight married couples, but occasionally the income has proved insufficient to support the full number, and some of the rooms have been kept vacant. Each inmate receives 6s. per week, $1\frac{1}{2}$ tons of coal annually, and a coat or cloak every second year.

The Haven of Rest. Almost next door to the fore-going is the ornate structure known as "The Haven of Rest." It is a series of almshouses erected by Mr. George Herring of Bridge House in 1895 for those who, through misfortune, found themselves reduced in circumstances. Here is comfortable provision for twelve married couples, who, amidst surroundings of refinement and tranquillity, may end their days in peace. Under a sun dial in the centre of the front lawn were interred on 30th November, 1906, the cremated remains of the Founder. The Charity is privately administered in accordance with directions given by Mr. Herring.

CHAPTER XVIII.

ROUND ABOUT.

OWEVER much or little Maidenhead may have touched or moulded England's national life, it is the centre of a district rich in names of national significance, political, social, and literary.

Windsor, in the stones of whose castle is written the whole story of English history from William I. to the present day, and Eton, in whose class rooms many of the greatest of England's sons were trained, and in whose playing fields the battle of Waterloo may, or may not, have been won, are both well within a six mile radius from Maidenhead. A few miles north-west lies Lady Place, once the stately home of the Lovelaces, in whose secret chambers and subterranean vaults were held those meetings and conclaves which did so much to ensure the downfall of the Stuarts and the triumph of William of Orange. Nearer is Bisham Abbey, where Warwick the king-maker was buried, and where Elizabeth spent three years as a prisoner in the custody of Sir Thomas Hoby. A few miles to the south-west is Shottesbrook, the Stuart stronghold, and the refuge of the non-jurors. Here dwelt Hearne, the Antiquary, and Francis Cherry, that man of a beautiful spirit, who would have nothing on his tombstone but "Hic jacet peccatorum maximus,"--and there it is to this

day, " Here lies the chief of sinners." Here,
too, the friend of Cherry, lived and died that
uncompromising non-juror and miracle of learning, Dr. Dodwell, whose strange ideas about the
soul not being naturally immortal, but becoming
so in baptism, are amusingly set forth in
Macaulay's history.

Not a great way off is Stoke Poges, where
rest the remains of the mother of the poet Gray,
who commemorated her in that oft-quoted and
touching epitaph, where he tells how of all her
children " one only had the misfortune to sur-
vive her"; and where he won for himself death-
less fame by his immortal " Elegy in a Country
Churchyard." Nearer still is Marlow, where
Shelley lived and wrote; and Down Place, where
linger memories of Jacob Tonson, publisher of
Dryden's works, keeper of open house for men
of letters, founder of the Kit-Cat Club, and,
when he one day put the screw on too tightly,
victim of Dryden's powers of satire, who, with
the message, " Tell the dog that he who wrote
this can write more," sent Tonson the three
famous lines :—

> " With leering look, bull-faced and freckled fair,
> With two left legs, with Judas-coloured hair,
> And frowsy pores that taint the ambient air."

COOKHAM.

Three miles to the north lies Cookham, which
gives its name to the ancient parish which took
in all Maidenhead on the north side of the Bath
Road. Formerly a market town, with tolls
valued in the Domesday Survey at the then

large sum of twenty shillings, it is now merely
a riverside village, a well known and popular
resort for boating and fishing. The Church
down by the river is of Norman parentage,
though its ivy-clad tower, so picturesque a feature
in the landscape, was not erected till 1500. In
the churchyard rest the remains of the restless
John Dawson, the Chaplain whose conflicts with
the Maidenhead Corporation in the days of
Charles I. have been recorded in a former chapter, and here too is all that is mortal of Frederick
Walker, the popular Associate of the Royal
Academy, who was taken away in the very prime
of his days. Brasses, as interesting as they are
numerous and varied, commemorate names that
live in neighbouring localities as given to, or
derived from, those commemorated. Here are the
Babhams of Babham End, where the old London
Road once crossed the river near Cookham before
Maidenhead bridge had seen the light. Here is
the tomb of the Monkedens who once held the
site, if not the house, called Monkendons
formerly standing in Maidenhead High Street.
Here, under an altar-tomb, lies Robert Peck, an
official in the Court of Henry VI., and here, too,
the genius of Flaxman perpetuates the memory
of another Maidenhead worthy, Sir Isaac Pocock.

CLIVEDEN.

Between Cookham and Maidenhead Bridge
stretches one of the finest reaches of the whole
of the river Thames. Broad green pasture
meadows mark the Berks shore, while on the

Bucks side are the steep slopes of a richly-wooded and lofty hill, crowned by two stately mansions. One of these is Cliveden, which looks out from its terrace on spacious lawns, gay with beautiful flowers, across the woods to the river winding at their feet, and then far away for miles and miles across country, altogether perhaps as glorious a view as any in England. Who can look on Cliveden without recalling Pope's line :—

" The bower of wanton Shrewsbury and love "?

There had been a duel fought at Barn Elms. George Villiers, the spendthrift Duke of Buckingham and profligate boon companion of Charles II., with Holmes and "one Jenkins"—so Pepys puts it—fought with the Earl of Shrewsbury, Sir John Talbot, and "one Bernard Howard," and all about my Lady Shrewsbury, and all the time that estimable personage stood by, disguised as a page, and held the Duke of Buckingham's horse while he ran his sword through her husband's body. This done, she and the Duke repaired to Cliveden, where the presence of the rightful mistress of the mansion being an inconvenience, a coach was ordered for her and she was dismissed to her father.

Cliveden had been purchased of the old county family of Manfield by Buckingham, but before the mansion was fully completed he had run through his property, and been reduced to that miserable condition which Pope has immortalised :—

" On once a flock bed, but repaired with straw,
With tape-tied curtains, never meant to draw ;
The George and Garter dangling from that bed
Where tawdy yellow strove with dirty red,

Great Villiers lies—alas! how changed from him,
That life of pleasure, and that soul of whim.
Gallant and gay in Cliveden's proud alcove
The bower of wanton Shrewsbury and Love;
Or just as gay at Council in a ring
Of mimicked statesmen and their merry King.
No wit to flatter left of all his store,
Or fool to laugh at, which he valued more,
There, victor of his health, his fortune, friends,
And fame, this lord of useless thousands ends."

For a time Cliveden was rented by Frederick,
Prince of Wales, son of George II., and father
of George III. Duller than his son, and as
profligate as his father, this prince died as he
lived, despised and unrespected. One thing may
nevertheless be put to his credit, he was the
patron and friend of Thomson, the poet, who was
a frequent guest at Cliveden. Here on August
1st, 1740, was produced his masque of "Alfred,"
a work which has been saved from oblivion by
the fact that it contained the well-known ode
"Rule Britannia." Set to music by Dr. Arne,
its stirring words and rousing melody were
first heard on "Cliveden's classic grounds."
Cliveden has passed successively into the
hands of George, Earl of Orkney, one of Young
Marlborough's Generals; Sir George Warrender,
who bought it for £3,500; Sir John Warrender;
the Duchess of Sutherland, Mistress of the
Robes to Queen Victoria, who often visited her
there; the Duke of Westminster; Mr. Astor;
and Viscount Astor.

Cary's Itinery for 1798 bids the traveller,
arrived at Maidenhead Bridge, look upstream
and note the "ruins of Cliveden." But though
Cliveden has been twice burned down, these

hardly be the ruins of fire, for the first fire was in 1751, 47 years before, and is usually attributed to a servant maid reading in bed in those good old times when beds were hung round as closely as possible with all manner of curtains and hangings. The second fire was during Sir John Warrender's tenure in 1849, but the origin of this calamity was never known certainly. It is believed to have been caused by a plumber. The present building had for its architect Sir Charles Barry, who also designed the Houses of Parliament. It is built in the Italian style, and is one of the most familiar, as it is one of the most beautiful, features in the landscape.

TAPLOW COURT.

Adjoining Cliveden are the lands and grounds of Taplow Court, the stately home where the latest of Maidenhead's High Stewards has on several occasions entertained his Sovereign. Originally, Taplow Church stood close to the site of the present mansion, and the windows on one side do still look out directly into the old graveyard. Here there is a large Saxon tumulus, which was opened some years since under the personal direction of Mr. James Rutland, F.R.G.S., of Taplow. The searchers were well rewarded. The results of the find are preserved in the British Museum, and include glass vessels, remains of costly and highly decorated raiment, and some gold jewels, one of the latter being the finest of its kind ever discovered.

BOULTER'S LOCK.

Close by Taplow Court is Boulter's Lock, unquestionably the most famous spot on the Thames, the "pulse of the river," as it has been called. ' Known all over the world as the picturesque entrance gate to one of the very finest reaches of the "River of Pleasure," its glories have been depicted by the artist, its crowds of brilliantly-dressed pleasure-seekers have over and over again been described by journalists, while probably no book has been published on the Thames for years past which has not referred to it. Half in the borough and half out of it, Boulter's Lock has repeatedly been traversed by the mace on boundary perambulations. As the centre of up-river traffic, over 1,400 craft, big and little, have been known to pass through it in a single day.

But who was Boulter? and why should he have a Lock? The question has often been asked. Gentle reader, Boulter was not a person at all. To "bolt" is to perform one of the operations of milling, and a "bolter" is a miller. This is not the lock of Mr. Boulter, it is "the miller's lock." Formerly a brewery stood next to the mill, one of the partners in which was Mr. Bell. In process of time, Bell's brewery was acquired by Messrs. Fuller, and removed to the centre of the borough, and when a new hotel rose near to the same, the original proprietor's name was perpetuated in the sign of the "Bell" Hotel.

Boulter's Lock, now on the Berks bank of the river, formerly stood on the Bucks shore, but prior to that, some hundred and fifty years ago, traffic was accommodated in very primitive style. Above the weir is a bar, and when a barge had to pass up the river it was customary to pull up the small gates at the bar and haul the barge through with main force. The lot of a barge-man was not always a happy one in those days.

BRAY.

One mile to the south of Maidenhead is Bray, and just as Cookham included in its ancient parish all of Maidenhead north of the Bath Road, so Bray claimed for its ancient parish all that lay on the south. Bray, like Cookham, was a royal manor, the proof of which statement is in a document of 22nd May, 2 Charles I., a copy of which is preserved in the Cookham Court Rolls. " The Lordships or Manors of Cookham and Bray with their appurtenances in the County of Berks are of the ancient Demesne of the Crown of England as hath been found and appeared by a certain Certificate thereof made by the Lord Treasurer, Chamberlains, and Barons of the Court of Exchequer by the Command of the Lady Elizabeth late Queen of England sent and transmitted into our Court of Chancery." Bray was also a Hundred, both manor and hundred being co-extensive with the parish, and including five subordinate manors, viz. : Creswells or Philberts, Lowbrooks, Foxleys, Stroud or Staver-tons, and Cruchfield, and also the five "reputed" manors of Hendons, Moores, Ockholt, or Ock-wells, Ives, and Shoppenhangers. It is generally

C.C.R.

supposed to have derived its name from the British tribe of the Bibroci, but it is its associations with its famous, or notorious, vicar which has given that name its world-wide notoriety. In his "Worthies," Fuller states that the reverend gentleman was one Symon Symonds, and proceeds, "The vivacious vicar thereof living under Henry VIII., King Edward VI., Queen Mary, and Queen Elizabeth; was first a Papist, then a Protestant, then a Papist, and then a Protestant again. He had seen some martyrs burnt (two miles off) at Windsor, and found this fire too hot for his tender temper. This vicar being taxed by one for being a turn-coat and an inconsistent changeling, said "Not so. I always keep my principle, which is this— 'To live and die the Vicar of Bray.' " The Vicar lives not only in the pages of Fuller, but in a song which bids fair to hand on the memory of his achievements to many generations yet to come. But the song does not quite agree with Fuller as to the date of its hero. It starts much later, in fact in the reign of Charles II., and carries him on through the days of James, William, and Anne, to the Georges. In date Fuller is to be preferred, but the sentiment of this accommodating clergyman cannot better be summed up than in the words of the chorus :—

> " For this is law I will maintain
> Until my dying day, sir,
> That whatever King doth reign,
> I'll be the Vicar of Bray, sir."

In Gorham's List of the Vicars, Symon Symonds is said to have been instituted on

March 14th, 1522-3, and to have been followed by Simon Dillin, who died in 1565. Gough, in his "Berkshire," gives this latter gentleman the credit for what Fuller ascribes to his predecessor. Whichever of these was the "versatile Vicar," it is said he resided in the rooms above the Lych-gate, on the south-east of the churchyard. This gate is a splendid example of an ancient porch, massively timbered, and bearing the date 1448. It was presented to the parish in 1839, through the munificence of the Rev. Walter Levett, is vested in trustees, and bids fair to stand for long a priceless memorial of the past.

Bray church dates from 1293, though a previous edifice had existed long before, and is mentioned in Domesday Book. The old church used to be repaired from funds raised by a "voluntary assessment," but as the men of Bray seem to have had a strange antipathy to such things, a weakness their successors have not wholly shaken off, however voluntary might have been the assessment, the payments got sadly in arrear; "wherefore it is commanded to the beadle [of the manor] that he go with the said Churchwardens diligently to raise the said assessment from those who refuse to pay it." So runs the old document, and doubtless the money came in, for the old church was then taken down, and the nave, west end, basement of chancel, and other portions of the present building date from this time. About 1400 the tower was erected, and it was the same date that saw the building of the Chapel of All Saints, at the east end of the south aisle, which was then, or subsequently, balanced by the Chapel of St. Nicholas at the east end of the North aisle. The Church has repeatedly fallen into the hands of cleaners and restorers, and many of its ancient features are gone or altered. The handsomely carved oak rood-screen is no more. The royal arms, once fixed to the screen, vanished at the Commonwealth. Mural paintings and decorations have been covered with whitewash, or pierced through for the erection of memorial tablets. The remains of a black-letter copy of Fox's Book of Martyrs, of the time of Queen Elizabeth, still exist in the vestry, an illustration of the culpable way in which ancient treasures are allowed to perish. The font, which dates from the time of Charles I., is said to be " the latest bid of pure Gothic in England before the Victorian revival." The Church is unusually rich in brasses and monuments, prominent amongst which are those of William Goddard, the founder of the Bray Almshouses; and John Rixman, the " charity " of whose loving wife still encourages the boys of Bray and Maidenhead in ways of learning and virtue. When the Church was last restored and the corbels of the new arches were carved, the features of Samuel Wilberforce, the Bishop of the Diocese, J. E. Austen Leigh, the Vicar, and M. Littleton, caretaker, were all faithfully reproduced, but Mrs. Bushnell, pew opener, caretaker and cleaner, lost her chance, as her poke bonnet, in which she insisted on being represented, did not lend itself to art, and she pointedly declined, as she put it, to be depicted in a night-cap!

On the north side of the churchyard stands an ancient Chauntry Chapel, certainly as old as the oldest part of the Church. In 1683 it was adapted to the purposes of a school, and here some ten years later Thomas Hearne of White Waltham, known in after years as the celebrated antiquary, received his early education.

In Bray village is Jesus Hospital, those picturesque Almshouses erected in 1623-28, pursuant to the will of their founder, William Goddard, and known all over the world to-day as forming the background in Frederick Walker's beautiful picture, "The Harbour of Refuge."

Bray is said to be the only church which has ever had its ringers go on strike. This happened, however, in August, 1876, during the Vicar's absence. A "machine" was in the meantime promptly introduced to ring the bells, and the incident brought the following jeu-d'esprit from the pen of a gentleman, who, under the pseudonym of "Scrutator," was a frequent contributor to the local press at that time.

A "STRIKING" BLUNDER.

Too keen after pay,
The Ringers of Bray
Forsook their post of action;
But *Roger* the wise,
To their surprise,
Outwitted the Village faction.

With sinues and thought
So deftly he wrought,

And Fortune so befriended,
    It came to pass
    That a small wind-*lass*
Does well-nigh what those *men* did.

    What *they* could do,
    Machinery too
Achieves, to their scant liking;
    And since they struck
    They find (worse luck)
How *hammers* can be striking.

    And now they fret
    In a vain regret
That prudence was not stronger.
    While memory stands
    They may wring their hands,
But they'll ring *those bells* no longer!

OCKWELLS.

Ockwells (or Ockholt) Manor lies about two miles to the south of Maidenhead, and the old manor house is a splendid example of the half-timbered houses of the Middle Ages. It was built in the early part of the reign of Edward IV., about 1466, and has been copied and described in endless works on art and architecture. The Manor was held by the family of Norreys, and an entry in the Patent Rolls in the 52 Hen. III. (1267) tells how the King grants it to Richard de Norreys. The present manor house was built by Sir John Norreys, who held several high and important offices at Court under both Henry VI. and Edward IV., and was one of the original members of the Maidenhead Guild. It contains, as is usual with

Kerry.

Rot. Pat.

this class of house, a very fine and lofty hall, with a large oriel window and dais at one end, and a musicians' gallery at the other. The oriel window contains some exceedingly fine stained glass and interesting coats of arms. A disastrous fire in 1778 destroyed the Chapel, and subsequently for many years the place was allowed to go into ruinous dilapidation, but a generous and wise restoration has preserved nearly all the ancient features, and arrested the progress of decay.

NOEL'S LANE.

A lane which long marked the western boundary of the Borough, but which has been widened and improved into what is now known as Courthouse Road, derived its original name from the fact that Mr. Noel resided there, who wrote the verses containing the well-known couplet :

> " Rattle his bones over the stones,
> He's only a pauper that nobody ownes,"

which with other writings had such a marked influence in obtaining a more humane Poor Law.

MAIDENHEAD THICKET.

Maidenhead Thicket has frequently been referred to in the preceding pages. It lies due West of the town about a mile and a half distant, and is traversed by the great Bath Road. Leyland, writing in the days of Henry VIII., says of his journey from Maidenhead to

Twyford, "From Maidenhedde toun a ii miles
by a narrow wooddy way to the Frithe. And
so through the Frithe iii miles and more. And
there to Twyford, a praty tounlet a ii miles."
It would therefore seem that this great wood was
at least five miles in diameter. On the north it
joined on to Pinkneys Green and to the south it
stretched in the direction of Windsor Forest,
which it is said to have joined. This vast extent
of shelter was infested with robbers who from
very early times had realised its advantages as
a happy hunting ground or place of refuge.

From time to time the road was widened and
the trees and bushes were cut back to render
travelling less dangerous. References to this
appear in the State Papers of 39 Hen. III.
(1255) and again on 9th April, 1634. In the
Statute of 39 Elizabeth c. XXV. passed "for
enlarging the Statutes for following the Hue and
Cry," the hundred of Beynhurst, in which the
thicket stands, was specially exempted from
penalties where there was no voluntary default.

Cal. St. Pap. Dom.

The *Quarterly Review* some years ago gave
currency to a local tradition that in the reign
of Queen Elizabeth " the Vicar of Hurley, who
served the cure of Maidenhead, was allowed an
extra salary for the danger of passing the
thicket." The *Review* gives no authority for
this statement, and it is to be feared there is
none to give. It is a thankless task exploding
old traditions, but no evidence whatever has been
produced in favour of this one, and the facts of
the case point in another direction. Prior to the
dissolution of the Monasteries priests for the

Quarterly Review, No. 211.

Maidenhead chantry had been selected by the
Prior of Hurley, but there is not a tittle of proof
that then or afterwards the Vicar of Hurley ever
was responsible for the Maidenhead cure. After
the dissolution Hurley ceased to have any
official connection with the Maidenhead chapel.
And as in the reign of Queen Mary the
inhabitants, after being for some years without
a chaplain, took the election into their own
hands, and received from the Crown a grant of
£4 13s. 4d. towards his support, it is most
unlikely that in the subsequent reign of Elizabeth an outsider like the Vicar of Hurley should
have appeared on the scene. The whole subject
has been dealt with by Mr. Stephen Darby in
an article in the Berks, Bucks, and Oxon
Archæological Journal, where the view taken is
the one here regretfully advocated.

B.B.O.,
Vol. 211.
No. 3, p. 92.

Of the highwaymen and footpads of Maidenhead Thicket endless tales are told, some of
which have already been alluded to. The story
goes that one of these highwaymen was also an
ostler at the " Sun," who, after having robbed
the coaches on the thicket, used to meet them
at the inn, and condole with the travellers. One
day he was missing, and was eventually found
in the loft bleeding, and mortally wounded by a
passenger on the coach who now vainly looked
for his services.

The race-course on the Thicket has been
described in the chapter on " Sport." A grass
track may also be traced from the lane leading
from Waltham Siding to Woolley Farm. It
acquired its name of " Taylor's Track " from

an employé of Mr. Clark of Altwood, who at
the time held both Norden and Woolley Farms. Silver.
Taylor found it too much trouble to go a long
way round, so made the shorter " track " which
bears his name.

CHAPTER XIX.

CHANGES.

IF one of those travellers accustomed to visit Maidenhead in the days of George IV. could come back and take another look at the town, he would see some changes. Standing on Maidenhead Bridge and looking down stream, he would see for the first time Brunel's great railway bridge, and would learn with amazement that the same railway took us to London in half-an-hour, and that if anyone ever went there by road it was no longer in a coach but in a motor car that could cover the distance within an hour. Gazing up stream he would ask what were those monstrosities which disfigured the banks on the Bucks shore, and would be told they were gas works, from whence came a vapour used all round the district for lighting, heating and cooking. And if his eye was caught by certain tall pillars gracefully tapering to the top, he would learn something of the wonders of the third of that trio of powers—steam, gas, electricity—which have revolutionised the world since our traveller was last here.

Turning his steps to the town he would look, and look in vain, for the old toll gate with its two square white toll-houses, and he would probably wonder what has become of the "King's Arms" inn. If he chanced to see the borough water-cart at work he would muse on the way they did things in the old days, when water having been pumped into the gutter on Folly Hill, its downward course was stopped by a piece of matting, and a man with a wooden scoop would throw the water into the road, and woe betide the careless passer-by. In the Salters' Almshouses he would recognise an old landmark, but the "Haven of Rest" would be a novelty. The Moor he would recognise, and perhaps the sight of a round-about in an adjoining field would call up memories of fair days, when any number of booths, stalls, and marvels, crowded the place and stretched all up the High Street, turning the whole town into a perfect Babel with the shouting of the vendors and the lowing of cattle, and he would hear with interest that these same wondrous fairs continued till past the middle of the nineteenth century.

At the Chapel Arches our Traveller would find the old Chapel of St. Andrew and St. Mary had vanished from the middle of the street, after standing there for five centuries and a half, and taken up its abode on its present site. The "Bear," too, he would see in a new position— no longer on the east side of the road next the Town Hall. The "Bull" and Ives Place Estate he would look for, but instead he would see a new road, a host of new houses, and what would astonish him most of all, a handsome Public Library. He would miss the old forge opposite the "Red Lion," and great would be his surprise at the Town Hall to see a handsome Bank on the site of the old "Bear," a

good road leading south past a fire-brigade
station—a thing he never saw or dreamed of
seeing in Maidenhead—and Market Street
superseding the narrow little lane once known
as Pitt's or Sheppard's Lane, looking in his
eyes so broad and spacious that he would
wonder greatly to hear people saying that it was
not broad enough and that the corner house on
the west side must come down to make a good
turning. "Why," he would say, "half of it
is down already. It was old Tull's public
house, and you cut it in two with your widening. Look how narrow the corner shop and the
meat shop are!" And as he looked round he
would ask, "Where are all the little houses that
used to be next the Town Hall? And where is
that little one next the Bank, where young
Rickman was born, who became so famous in
architecture? Though, by the way, that was
not the bank in my day; the bank was at the
east corner of Market Street."

Queen Street would utterly confound him. He
would look in vain for the tortuous windings of
Pope's Lane, and the low-roofed houses, once
covered with roses, where lived Zerubbabel
Wyvill, organist of St. Mary's, music-master in
chief to the community, writer of the music for
patriotic songs, and composer of the old tune
"Eton"; and Butterfield, another architect who,
like Rickman, achieved distinction. But for
Peter Pope himself, landlord of the " Hand and
Flowers," our traveller would not enter the
present house with that name to find him, for
the original was about half the size, and fronted

Marginal notes:

An Act for
Widening
Pitt's Lane,
19 Geo. 2.

Silver.

No. 61 to 67 High Street as it appeared in 1864.

From a drawing in the possession of P. D. Thompson, Esq.

the High Street. As for all beyond Pope's Lane, and to the south of the High Street generally, it was all fields and twisting lanes.

Proceeding up the High Street, our traveller would find the imposing premises of Messrs. Webber, and the Westminster Bank occupying the site of the renowned "Greyhound." The splendid business premises on the south side would baffle him completely, nor would his astonishment be lessened as he gazed at the large "Sixpenny Emporium" of Woolworths, occupying the ground where once stood Monkendons with its flight of stone steps, its fore-courtyard, its heavy iron railings, and its luxurious lilac trees, once the home of James Payne, the Recorder, and moved by him from White Waltham with the help of some of his friends, stimulated thereto, so it is said, by the Recorder's generous " hospitality." He would smile as he greeted once more the medallion on No. 95, and would (probably) say, " Yes, there's His Most Gracious Majesty, George IV.," but the sight of the Wesleyan Chapel would stagger him hopelessly. To say nothing of his astonishment at Methodists dwelling anywhere except in back alleys, he would exclaim, "Where is the cabbage patch that stood where the chapel is? Where is Silver. the watch-box from which old Collins used nightly to issue, and make darkness hideous by his crying the hours? And where is the weigh- Maid. J. 96. ing machine that used to be in the Braywick Road just outside the White Horse? " Where indeed? The " Sun," no longer an inn, still occupies the corner of Marlow Road, but it is needless to say our traveller would hardly recognise that corner, and would look a long time before he found the " Two Brewers," once the occupant of the east side.

Should he journey along King Street he would find business premises occupying the site of William Frowd's humble forge. Good old Billy Frowd! He could make music as well as horse-shoes; he played the cornet, was leader of a brass band, and a prominent musician at St. Mary's, where also made music another gentle-man who dwelt hard by, John Kay, and who did not always see eye to eye with Mr. Frowd—which was not remarkable, for Mr. Kay had a defective sight, as well as an unfortunate limp-ing gait. So the wits of the day parodied a verse of a hymn then popular, but now long since dropped from every hymn-book, and sang :—

> " Behold how singers disagree,
> Billy Frowd and Johnny Kay.
> One doth his bugle-horn proclaim,
> The other is both blind and lame."

We will not ask our visitor to go farther south, for all will be new and strange to him. In his day there was hardly a house in the whole district. But he ought to take a peep on the north side, if only to walk down West Street, or Back Lane, as he would call it, and note that the great ditch which once went all down one side has gone, and its evil odours with it. If he penetrate further, instead of a farm he will see Kidwell's Park, and instead of a broad expanse of fields, St. Luke's Church and all the streets and houses that make up Norfolk Park. If he visit East Street, Boyn Hill, and Gordon

Road, he will ask in wonder " What are all these palatial buildings with their extensive grounds and splendid equipment?" and will learn with amazement that they are the successors, the development, of that modest little school house, later on turned into cottages, but now entirely removed, which was set up in the old gravel pit at the Folly in the last years of George III. Standing opposite that same Folly, though the strange buildings of Cook's Folly are now no more, he would see houses stretching in all directions. Berry Villa, once the last house between Maidenhead and the " Coach and Horses " beyond Maidenhead Thicket, would seem but the beginning of a long line of houses which, with little intermission, stretches along the Bath Road to beyond Punt Hill. And so all round. And when he had heard of Churches, Halls, Clubs, Baths, Hospitals, Libraries, and, what would probably be to him the crowning wonder of all, a series of bacteria beds and a complete sanitary system which has made the town one of the healthiest in the country, he would probably acknowledge that Maidenhead had moved a little since the good old days.

APPENDIX A.

Various Spellings of the Name.

1248	18 Aug.	Maydehuth	Charter Rolls	Hen. III.
1274	29 Jan.	Maidenheth	Rot. Pat.	
,,	4 Mar.	Maidenhethe	Rot. Cl.	Ed. I.
1282	23 Jan.	Maydenhaith	Rot. Pat.	
1286	28 Ap.	Maydenhach	Rot. Cl.	Ed. I.
1292	15 July	Maydenhacche	Rot. Cl.	Ed. I.
1293	12 June	Maydenheche	Rot. Cl.	Ed. I.
1297	4 Dec.	Maydeneth	Rot. Pat.	Ed. I.
1313	29 Ap.	Maydenhethe	Rot. Pat.	
1318	3 Aug.	Maydenach	Rot. Cl.	Ed. II.
1320	28 Feb.	Maydenhide	Rot. Cl.	Ed. II.
1331	23 Jan.	Maydenhethe	Rot. Pat.	
1334	24 Sep.	Maydenhuthe	Rot. Cl.	Ed. III.
1340	6 Ap.	Maydenhuth	Rot. Cl.	Ed. III.
1347	20 Aug.	Maydenhith	Rot. Cl.	Ed. III.
1351	23 Jan.	Maydenhyth	Rot. Cl.	Ed. III.
1353	27 Ap.	Maydenhithe	Rot. Cl.	Ed. III.
1410	(circ.)	Mideheet	Original French translation of the Chronicle of the betrayal and death of Rich. II.	
		Mardeohee	Another French translation of the same.	
		Mihet	,,	
		Mendeult	,,	
		Mèdehoe	,,	
1463	28 June	Medynhith	Rot. Pat.	
1522	7 Jan.	Maidenhith	Cal. Letters and Papers Hen. VIII.	
1528		Medonhedd	,,	
1531	Sep.	Maidenhed	,,	
1536	29 Nov.	Maydynhyth	,,	

1540	22 July	Maydenhache	Cal. Letters and Papers Hen. VIII.
1541	20 Jan.	Maydenhed	,,
1584	Nov.	Maidenheath	Dom. St. Pap.
1618	8 June	Maydenhead	K. 122.
1720	20 June	Meadenhead	K. 136.
1724	3 Dec.	Maidenhead	J. 87.

APPENDIX B.

Where is Maidenhead?

Latitude.	51° 31′ North.
Longitude.	0° 43′ West.
Altitude:	At Town Hall (surface) 90 feet above sea level.
Distance from	Hyde Park Corner by the Bath Road, 26 miles.
,, ,,	London Bridge by River Thames, 50 miles.
,, ,,	Paddington Station, by G.W.R., 24¼ miles.
County:	Berkshire.

Parliamentary Division: Windsor.

Parish: Maidenhead. Prior to 15th October, 1894, partly in Parish of Cookham and partly in Parish and Hundred of Bray.

Public Assistance: Windsor Division — Maidenhead Section.

County Court: District of Berkshire held at Windsor and Maidenhead.

Local Authority for Elementary Education: Maidenhead.

,, ,, ,, Higher ,, Berkshire.

In Area of	Uxbridge & District Gas Company.
,,	Maidenhead Waterworks Company.
,,	Maidenhead Corporation Electric Light Undertaking.
Anglican:	Province of Canterbury.
,,	Diocese of Oxford (Salisbury prior to 1836).
,,	Archdeaconry of Berks.
,,	Rural Deanery of Maidenhead.
Roman Catholic:	Diocese of Portsmouth.
Congregational:	Berks, South Oxon and South Bucks Congregational Union.
Methodist:	Second London District.
Baptist:	Berks Baptist Association.
Society of Friends:	Berks and Oxon Quarterly Meeting.
Salvation Army:	West London Division.
Independent Order of Oddfellows: (M.U.)	Great Marlow District. Queen of England Lodge.
Do. Grand United:	Pride of Maidenhead Lodge.
Ancient Order of Foresters:	Bucks and Middlesex District Court Prince Albert.
Independent Order of Rechabites:	Berks, Bucks and Oxon District, Maidenhead Tent.

APPENDIX C.

Statistics for Michaelmas, 1930.

Area of Borough - - - - -	2,123 acres
Inhabited houses - - - - -	4,861
Uninhabited ,, - - - - -	88
Houses in course of erection - - -	14
Unreduced Rateable Value - -	£137,474

Reduced Rateable Value - - - £131,794
No. of Burgesses in Belmont Ward 2,519
     Boyne Hill Ward 1,909
     Oldfield Ward 1,387
     St. Mary's Ward 2,613
         —— 8,428
No. of Parliamentary Electors - - - 11,931

APPENDIX D.

Population.

Year.	Population.	Year.	Population.
1801	949	1881	8,219
1811	792	1891	10,607
1821	945	1901	12,980
1841	3,315	1911	15,218
1851	3,603	1921	16,730
1861	3,893	1931 (estimated)	18,000
1871	6,173		

APPENDIX E.

Mayors of Maidenhead.

1685	Vincent Pawlyn	92	Thos. Russell
	(by Charter)	93	Stephen Fisher
	Stephen Fisher	94	
	(elected in Sept.)	95	Charles Spratley
86	Geo. Russell	96	Wm. Keene
87	Richd. Widmore	97	Richard Baker
88	Wm. Keene	98	Giles Clifford
89	Ed. White	99	Robert Beaver
1690	Richd. Baker	1700	Geo. Russell
91	Ed. Browne	01	Ed. Browne

02	Stephen Fisher	1740	John Butterfield
03	Sampson Urlin	41	Matthew Geary
04	Wm. Spratley	42	John Johnson
05	Thos. Robins	43	Henry Emblin
06	Wm. Hale	44	George Heelas
07	Joseph Fellows	45	Richard Withall
08	Wm. Smith	46	John Hall
09	John Langton	47	Robert Goldsmith
1710	Ch. Spratley	48	John Gaskins
11	Thos. Wastell	49	Matthew Geary
12	Wm. Keen	1750	Edward Cole (left
13	Howell Powell		Maidenhead)
14	Wm. Goddard		John Medden
15	Thos. Luff	51	James Adams
16	Stephen Goldsmith	52	William Rose
17	Robert Bever	53	James Hudson
18	Wm. Spratley	54	William Grove
19	Thos. Robins	55	John Gould
1720	Henry Evans	56	John Butterfield
21	Wm. Hale	57	Henry Emblin
22	Wm. Smith	58	George Heelas
23	John Langton	59	Henry Lovegrove
24	James Hall	1760	Richard Withall
25	Thos. Darvale	61	John Hall
26	Wm. Goddard	62	Robert Goldsmith
27	Henry Evans	63	James Adams
28	Thos. Luff	64	William Rose
29		65	John Lawes
1730	John Butterfield	66	James Hudson
31	Matthew Geary	67	John Clark
32	Moses Jeffery	68	John Gould
33	Richard Hobbs	69	John Boult
34	John Johnson	1770	Henry Lovegrove
35	Henry Emblin	71	James Attlee
36	James Adams	72	Henry Emblin
37	William Hall	73	Richard Taylor
38	John Mercy	74	Aspin Taylor
39	William Grove	75	John Butterfield

76	Abraham Darby
77	John Langton
78	John Clark
79	John Gould
1780	James Atlee
81	Francis Justice
82	Thos. Smith
83	Thos. Devas
84	Giles Goldsmith
85	William Parker
86	Hugh Penfold
87	Giles Taylor
88	Joseph Clark
89	Henry Seymour
1790	John Butterfield
91	Abraham Darby
92	Francis Justice
93	Thomas Cullern
94	John Langton (declined, paid fine)
	Thomas Smith
95	Thomas Devas
96	Abraham Darby, jun.
97	Wm. Parker
98	Jemmy Wells
99	Joseph Clark
1800	Henry Seymour
01	William Poulton
02	William Stroud
03	John Butterfield
04	Austin Sherwood
05	William Piggott
06	William Aldridge
07	Richard Lovegrove
08	Thomas Smith
09	John Langton (declined, paid £50)
	Thomas Foster

1810	John Ebsworth
11	Richard Goulden
12	Thomas Groome
13	Lawrence Norman
14	Joseph Clark
15	Austin Sherwood
16	William Piggott
17	Richard Lovegrove
18	Thomas Smith (declined, paid £50)
	John Langton (declined, paid £50)
	John Ebsworth
19	Thomas Foster
1820	Thomas Groome
21	Lawrence Norman
22	Richard Goulden
23	Joseph Clark
24	William Piggott
25	Richard Lovegrove
26	John Langton (declined, paid £50)
	John Wade Witton
27	Robert Wyville
28	Thomas Groome
29	John Lewington
1830	James Smith
31	Robert Nicholson
32	John E. Langton
33	Richard Goulden
34	Charles Williams
35	Joseph Clark. First after the Municipal Corporation Act, Elected 1 Jan, 1836
36	John E. Langton
37	William Payn
38	W. J. Ward

39	John Green Bishop
1840	James Swallow
41	Richard Lovegrove
42	George Mills
43	Henry Spratley
44	John Higgs
45	John Higgs
46	J. E. Langton
47	Benjamin Bellis
48	William Lock
49	William Lock
1850	Charles Cooper
51	Charles Cooper
52	J. E. Langton
53	Robert Andrew Stevens
54	E. W. Mackie
55	H. H. Durrant
56	J. D. M. Pearce
57	J. D. M. Pearce
58	Caleb Colman
59	Caleb Colman
1860	Benjamin Bellis
61	Benjamin Bellis
62	J. D. M. Pearce
63	Joseph Smith
64	Joseph Smith
65	H. H. Durrant
66	Robert Nicholson
67	Robert Nicholson
68	Samuel Moffat Preece
69	Samuel Moffatt Preece
1870	Robert Walker
71	Robert Walker
72	Richard Silver
73	H. H. Durrant
74	H. H. Durrant
75	E. W. Mackie
76	William Woodbridge
77	Richard Silver
78	Richard Illsley
79	Richard Illsley
1880	Richard Illsley
81	William Berry Farr
82	William Berry Farr
83	Charles W. Cox
84	William Lovering
85	William Woodbridge
86	H. H. Durrant
87	E. W. Mackie
88	Charles W. Cox
89	J. D. M. Pearce
1890	J. D. M. Pearce
91	J. F. Simpson
92	Ernest Gardner
93	William Withnall
94	John Bugden
95	William Henry Grenfell
96	William Henry Grenfell
97	Charles W. Cox
98	John Truscott
99	Edwin Hewitt
1900	David Wilton
01	William Ferguson Good
02	James Edward Pearce
03	Benjamin Hobbis
04	Benjamin Hobbis
05	John Wesley Walker
06	Charles William Cox
07	Arthur Upson

08	David Bidmead	21	Thomas William Stuchbery
09	Francis W. Porter	22	Thomas William Stuchbery
1910	William Ferguson Good	23	Thomas William Stuchbery
11	Edward Norket	24	Henry Vaisey
12	Charles Thos. Chamberlain	25	Lucian Robert Frederic Oldershaw
13	Edward Norket		
14	Edward Norket	26	Charles Thomas Chamberlain
15	Charles William Cox		
16	Charles William Cox	27	Charles William Cox
17	Charles William Cox	28	William Archer
18	Charles William Cox	29	Ernest B. Norris
19	Thomas William Stuchbery	1930	Ernest B. Norris
1920	Thomas William Stuchbery		

APPENDIX F.

The Borough Boundary.

The Borough Boundary is set forth on the Ordnance Map and has been verified by repeated perambulations. One of such perambulations took place on 16th September, 1909, in the mayoralty of Mr. David Bidmead. The following paragraphs are extracted from the official Report prepared by the Town Clerk.

The perambulation commenced from a stone on the west side of Cookham Road, opposite Boulter's Lock. Nails were found in the fence immediately above the stone, and a new nail 'marked " D.B. 1909," was driven in by the Mayor, and tapped with the Mace.

The Mace was then passed across the road and over the fence of Boulter's Lock, a nail being driven in the piles at the foot of the fence. The party then boarded Mr.

Bond's Launch, which was waiting in the Lock, the Mace
being passed over the Launch to the other side, where
a small party landed and conveyed the Mace over the
hedge of the Lock premises and on in a direct line through
grounds belonging to Mr. Joseph Fuller, to the entrance
to Mr. J. P. Stearn's house, thence through the front
entrance into the drawing-room, and out through the
casement to a point exactly opposite. The Mace was then
handed over the wall to Mr. G. Bond, who was in a punt
below, and conveyed by him in a direct line to the Launch,
which was moored in mid stream just below Boulter's
Lock.

The Party now proceeded down the centre of the main
stream to a point opposite premises on the Bucks shore
formerly occupied by Mr. E. Andrews as a boathouse, but,
now occupied by Mr. Willoughly. Here the Mace was
landed on the Eyot about 30 feet from the southern end,
and conveyed thence across the back water to the entrance
to the premises above described, which entrance it was
stated was built over what was originally a ditch. A nail
was driven in the camp-shedding under the steps of these
premises and the party proceeded through a passage way
(built over the before mentioned ditch), bearing to the
right at the top end into a lavatory, where the Mace was
passed through a skylight and conveyed by the Assistant
Town Clerk along the adjoining wall, and through a
narrow space between the River Club and a house in the
occupation of Mr. Thurston, to the road adjoining, where
a stone was found. (On previous occasions the perambulations commenced from this spot.)

From here the road was crossed in an oblique south-
easterly direction to the Office of Skindle's Hotel. A few
of the party entered, and found a cross on the south wall
of the room; this was tapped with the Mace, which was
then carried round to the other side of the wall in the
dining-room, and tapped on that part of the wall opposite
the mark referred to. The room was then crossed to the
second window from the west on the south side of the

house, out of which the Mace was passed, and several of the party also passed through the window, and under the outside of the sill a cross was found.

The Bath Road was then crossed in a direct line from the window to the west side of the road leading to the " Sounding Arch," the line followed being the west side of the carriageway (the pathway being in the Borough) to a stone at the " Shooting-on-Point," situate 137 feet south from Bond's Boathouse, and 386 feet north from the " Sounding Arch." This stone, it was stated, marked the boundary of the Corporation Fishery.

An old stone marked " CORP. W. 1870 " was found imbedded in the bank at this spot, and it was ordered to be recovered and re-erected near the existing stone.

From here the Mace was conveyed in a direct line by the aid of a punt to the Launch which had been anchored in 'mid stream. Proceeding down the centre of the stream to a point nearly opposite Mr. Woodhouse's Boathouse, some of the party landed on the east bank, and found a stone close to a Hawthorn bush, called the lower bush.

Alderman Cox explained that this stone did not mark the boundary, but marked the point opposite which the boundary ran, which point was the south east boundary of the Borough. The Mace was then conveyed in a punt in an oblique direction to the outlet of a small water-course on the south side of a house known as " Riverbank," in the centre of which stream a post was found containing several nails marking previous perámbulations, and a new one was driven. Proceeding up the stream to a foot-bridge known as Gaskins Bridge, in the centre post of this a nail was driven by the Mayor.

From here the Mace was conveyed by Thomas Harding under the north arch of a small brick bridge a few yards further west, in the centre beam of which nails were found, and a new one was driven by the Ex-Mayor. Proceeding along the south side of the stream, the boys beating the centre of the stream with their flags, to a point opposite the last elm tree on the north side thereof, a crossing was effected to the adjoining field, where two other large elm trees were found, in the last of which a nail was driven.

The Mace was then carried along the line of an old waterway to Bray Road, where it was discovered that the boundary stone on the west side of that road had been removed some 17 yards from its correct position, and it was ordered to be replaced.

Proceeding along the centre of the road leading to Braywick to the junction with Braywick Road, on the high brick wall surrounding Mr. Hibbert's property, were found several crosses and marks as follows: H.H.D. X 1856; H.H.D. X 1874; R.S. X 78; C.W.C. X 91; D.W. X 1901, to which was ordered to be added D.B. X 1909.

Crossing Braywick Road and continuing due west along the centre of Harvest Hill and Kimbers Lane, passing Kimbers House and "The Shepherd's Hut," to the junction of three roads running north, east and west, at the foot of an elm tree standing in the angle of the roads running north and west, which contained several nails, and in which another was driven, was found a stone denoting the south west boundary of the Borough, the marks on which were almost obliterated and ordered to be recut.

The centre of the road running north, known as Dog Kennel Lane, was traversed to a point opposite the Forresters' Arms, at the junction of the Cox Green Road, where several nails were found in the sign post, and another was driven, making six in all.

Continuing along the west side of the road until another open space was reached called Pope's Hole, a stone was found.

The Mace was then carried by Councillor Thompson along the ditch on the west side of the road until some cottages were reached, through the front gardens of which the boundary lay, and over which the Mace was passed to a stone at the entrance to the rear of a further row of cottages, the boundary passing between the cottages and the offices at the rear, thence to a stone in the wall of the

Great Western Railway, on which was ordered to be cut
" D.B. 1909." The party then climbed the embankment
by means of a ladder, and crossed the main line of the
Great Western Railway to a stone in a field on the north
side thereof, following the line of a ditch at the eastern
boundary of the field to a point seventeen feet from the
south-west corner of a house in the occupation of Mr.
Palmer adjoining " The Orchards," in the fence of which
a nail was driven. Scaling the fence the party crossed in
a direct line across the garden of the house to a wall adjoining Altwood Road, over which the Mace was passed. Here
marks of previous perambulations were found to which
was ordered to be added " D.B. X 1909."

The Mace was carried over Altwood Road, and over a
fence to a large willow tree, where nails were found, and
another ordered to be driven, then proceeding along the
east side of the garden which adjoins the " Plough " Inn,
and skirting some cottages, the party arrived at a high
wall dividing the garden from premises owned by Mr.
Filewood, known as " The Recess," and occupied by Mr.
Jamieson, on the south side of which a stone was ordered
to be placed bearing the initials of the Mayor and the date
subject to permission being obtained from the owner.

After surmounting the wall the party passed through the
garden of " The Recess " to a wall on the south side
thereof, but owing to the accumulation of ivy it was not
possible to find the nails driven in on previous occasions.
The Mace having been passed over this wall the party
entered the garden of premises owned and occupied by Mr.
O. Johnson where a nail was driven in a tree near the wall.
Proceeding in a northerly direction up the path of the
garden the party came across a well, in the upright of
which a nail was ordered to be driven in line with the
four existing nails.

The highway was now reached, where a stone was found.
A few feet north of the stone was a large elm tree in which
a nail was ordered to be driven.

Proceeding along the west side of the road three stones

were found at intervals where the road had been widened, the stone in the centre being buried in the road.

The Bath Road was now reached, and turning west a stone was found on the south side of the Bath Road opposite the entrance to Courthouse Lane, marking the western boundary, on which the Mace was tapped. Turning due north a stone was found on the west side of the entrance to Courthouse Lane. A nail was ordered to be driven in the tree immediately above the stone.

Keeping along the west side of Court house Lane as far as Mr. J. C. Wooton's house, Boyn Grove, the north east corner of the grounds was taken in. The Mace was passed over from the north east corner of the house to a post in which a nail was driven on the last perambulation, but which had been removed. It was ordered that a stone be placed at this spot. Crossing in a north westerly direction to the third elm tree on the north side of a new road, a stone was found. Keeping to the ditch on the west side of the road, the party emerged on to St. Mark's Road (formerly the old Henley Road), crossing the road to a stone marking the boundary at the south east corner of an old pit known as Joe Neighbour's Pit.

Keeping to the west side of Courthouse Lane the party arrived at a large elm tree standing in the angle of the road where it turns slightly to the right to the west of a cottage known as Crookfield Cot. In this tree it was ordered that a nail be driven and that a stone be erected at the foot thereof. Continuing along the western side of the road to the junction of Linden Avenue, and at a point where a burial path crosses Mr. Weall's fields, a stone was found denoting the north west boundary of the Borough.

Turning east, the party traversed the northern side of the path on the south side of the road, crossing Marlow Road to Harrow Lane, on the northern side of the entrance to which a stone was found. Continuing down Harrow Lane over the railway level crossing, the party arrived at the wall of the Harrow Inn where various marks were found, and the following ordered to be added, " D.B. X 1909."

The Mace was passed over the wall and across the garden to a point where the wall joins the house, where it was passed back over the wall, through the Bar of the Harrow Inn and out through the window on the east side, under which a stone was found. The road was then crossed in an oblique direction to the north east boundary of Laggan House, where numerous marks were found on the wall, and to which was ordered to be added " D.B. X 1909."

The Mace was then carried up a ladder and along the roof wall to the coach-house, on the north west and north east walls of which crosses were ordered to be cut with the initials of the Mayor and the date, near those at present existing.

From the latter point a descent was made into a paddock belonging to Miss Smith. At the point of descent crosses were found, and another ordered to be cut with initials and date. Passing along the eastern wall of Laggan House Garden a brick pier at the south east corner of the property was reached on which a cross was found.

Turning east along the north side of Moor Lane for a distance of 50 yards or thereabouts, two stones were found at the foot of a post in the fence, in which post several nails were discovered. One of the stones was ordered to be removed back to the foot of the brick pier at Laggan House before referred to.

The party continued along the north side of the road as far as Moor Cottage in the occupation of Mr. W. French, in one of the brick piers of the wall surrounding which were found marks of a previous perambulation. On this pier was ordered to be marked " D.B. X 1909." The Mace was then passed over the wall and across the garden to a wall on the north east side of the premises, where marks were discovered and others ordered to be cut. Passing over the wall to a cottage through which the Mace was carried, marks were ordered to be cut at the entrance and in the eastern wall, where existing marks were found. The Mace

having been tapped on both sides of the east wall of the
cottage through which the line of the boundary runs, the
party proceeded in a direct line across the moor to a stone
on the north side of a ditch.

From opposite the stone the Mace was carried along the
south side of a ditch to a gate, in the post of which a nail
was ordered to be driven.

A direct line was taken east across a stream and on
through fields until the party came to two large elm trees
in a field owned by Mr. Ernest Gardner, M.P., a few feet
from which a stone was found on which was ordered to
be cut " D.B. 1909."

In the second tree a nail which was almost overgrown
with bark was ordered to be cut clear, and another one
bearing the Mayor's initials and the date ordered to be
driven. Here a stone was found denoting the boundary
of the Ecclesiastical parish of St. Luke.

Proceeding still east, the party emerged on to a road
leading to Sheephouse Farm, at a point opposite the gate
of Ray Court, where a stone was found on the west side of
the road. Crossing the road a nail was driven into a post
of the fence, where one driven at the last perambulation
was found. The Mace was handed over the fence and the
party proceeded due east along the northern boundary of
a field until another stone was reached, then on to another
stone on the side of a ditch near Lock Mead Hole, then
turning due south and skirting the ditch until a point was
reached about 140 yards from Ray Mill Road where a stone
was found on the east side of the ditch. Here a crossing
was effected and a stone ordered to be placed on the west
side of the ditch opposite the one on the east side. Following a line due east the grounds of Mr. F. C. Burnett's house
were entered at a walnut tree, in which a nail was driven.
Crossing the grounds, and skirting the house on the south
side, the party reached a large sycamore tree situated in
the drive leading up to the house from Ray Mill Road,
being the fourth tree from the entrance gate, and being
situate close to the south west angle of the boundary wall

of the adjoining property known as Ray Mead Cottage. In this tree nails were found, and another ordered to be driven. The Mace was passed over the wall into the grounds of Raymead Cottage, thence due south for some 50 feet to a point opposite the garden path leading to the main entrance of the house. Instructions having been given for the marks " D.B. X 1909," to be placed on each side of the wall where the party crossed, and at the point 50 feet south thereof, the line of the garden path was followed over the grounds in a direct line to the stone from which the start was made.

APPENDIX G.

𝕽oll of 𝕳onour

Containing names of men of Maidenhead and District who laid down
their lives in the Great War, 1914-1918.

A. F. Ada
A. J. Aldridge
C. W. Aldridge
A. Alexander
W. Alexander
A. E. Allen
F. H. Allen
S. C. Ambrose
F. J. Anderson
W. G. Andrews
T. W. Angus
J. L. Ansell
T. L. Annes
P. W. Annetts
G. W. J. Arnett
C. E. Attwood
C. T. Austin
F. E. Austin
R. J. Austin
W. J. Austin
T. F. Ayers

F. W. Bailey
H. J. T. Baldwin
W. J. Bannister
H. H. Barford
F. W. Bartlett
B. E. Bates
R. J. Bates
H. H. Baylis
A. G. Beadell
J. J. Beckett
A. E. Beckley
S. E. Belcher
E. E. Bennett
G. D. Bennett
G. W. Bennett
J. C. Beesley
C. R. Betts
A. N. Bidmead
G. Bird
H. W. Bird
R. S. Bishop
W. H. Bissley
E. Bloomfield
G. A. Bloomfield
M. G. Bloomfield

W. H. Bloyce
C. Bolton
F. G. Bond
G. Bond
J. Boyd
G. Bradley
H. R. Bradley
F. H. Britten
W. Britten
S. Broadbent
F. Brooker
J. J. Brooker
J. Brooker
W. Burrow
A. J. Burrough
H. Bushell
F. J. Butler
E. E. Button
W. Buxton
A. T. Bye
L. J. Bye

J. F. Caines
O. D. Carew
A. Carter
E. Carter
W. J. Castell
M. F. Chamberlain
J. Chandler
W. Chitty
W. Chitty
A. C. Church
W. G. Church
E. G. Clark
C. Clarke
W. H. Clarke
G. Clilverd
G. Conboy
W. F. Coxhead
A. Crockford
W. Croft
N. Crosby
W. H. Crosby
F. H. Crouch
E. Cutler

T. G. Dale

W. J. Dale
F. Dalton
E. V. Darke
B. R. Davis
E. S. Davis
H. S. Dean
A. C. Dedman
H. Deller
G. J. Devonshire
A. Dicker
K. B. Ditton
E. C. Dobson
C. B. Dormer
H. W. Dovey
L. N. Dovey
F. Dray
C. Durrant
V. Durrant
G. A. Dyke

E. F. Eaton
G. Eaton
J. H. Eaton
A. Edwards
J. Edwards
C. H. Eggleton
J. A. W. Emberley

G. Furguson
J. E. Field
H. V. Fisher
S. Fisher
W. Fisher
W. G. Folley
R. Foster
W. Foster
G. Fryer

L. Gaines
C. Galpin
D. Garraway
F. George
G. H. T. Gibson
B. S. Gibbons
P. Gibbons
A. S. Gilder
F. T. Gilder

C. Godfrey
F. W. Godfrey
D. Goddard
E. Goebel
A. Goodall
J. A. Grant
N. A. Gray
F. W. Green
Hon. J. H. F. Grenfell, D.S.O.
Hon. G. W. Grenfell
W. Grey
F. T. Griffin
A. E. Grimmett
F. G. W. Groves
G. Groves
A. E. Grubb

E. Alfred Harding
E. Arthur Harding
R. P. Harker
A. J. Harris
G. J. Harris
R. Harris
S. Harris
A. H. Headington
J. W. Hedges
W. Hedges
R. R. Henry
G. Hodges
A. Holmes
W. J. Holland
G. A. Holloway
C. W. Homer
W. J. Hulcup
J. Hunt
W. E. Hunter
T. W. Hutton

G. H. Illsley
C. J. Ireland

A. Jackson
B. Jackson
C. Jackson
E. W. Jackson
E. P. Jackson
R. A. Jackson
C. A. Johannsen
L. E. Janes
H. F. E. Jones
J. T. Jones
W. H. Jones
D. Joynson

C. S. Kail
R. S. Kail

W. P. Kail
J. Keeley
G. W. King
H. King
W. H. H. Kinge

C. W. Lacey
W. Lambert
S. M. Lester
W. J. R. Lewis
M. Line
O. P. Lipscombe
W. Lipscombe
A. E. Littleton
H. Littleton

D. F. Mackay
J. E. Marks
F. Marshall
F. J. Maskell
R. G. Maskell
C. C. Mason
C. W. Mason-MacFarlane
A. M. McHard
A. McLean
F Meads
E. Mitchell
S. C. Mitchell
F. W. Moore
G. Moore
R. L. Moore
F. J. Muggridge
E. A. Myer
E. G. Mynett

F. E. Nash
P. Naylar
E. W. Neighbour
R. E. Neve
H. E. Newell
W. S. Newport
A. Nicholls
L. C. Nicholson, D.S.O.
S. Nightingale
E. Norkett
R. North
C. W. Nowell
W. J. Nuccoll

A. R. Outram
R. Owen
W. H. Owen

W. G. Palmer
G. H. Parker

A. Pavey
J. Parkin
W. H. Pert
A. J. Peters
J. H. Poole
R. H. Porter
T. T. Pryce, V.C.
F. Proctor
F. Pym, D.C.M.

E. A. Rackley
O. Read
G. C. Rhodes
C. W. M. Ricks
C. E. Richardson
H. Richmond
C. H. J. Ridgley
W. Ridler
W. H. Roadnight
A. F. Roberts
W. Roberts
R. F. Rockwell
F. E. M. Roe, D.C.M.
E. W. Rolfe
W. J. H. Rose

A. Sacks
J. H. Salmon, D.C.M.
A. H. Saunders
W. E. C. Saunders
A. K. Scott, D.C.M.
D. J. Scott
H. J. Scott
J. Setter
S. J. Setter
L. W. Seymour
S. H. Seymour
T. Seymour
C. H. Sharp
G. Shaw
J. W. Shelton
F. W. Shingleton
T. H. Shirvill
H. Shoebridge
W. H. Simmance
C. H. B. Slocock
L. A. N. Slocock
H. R. Smart
E. J. Smith
F. Smith
F. R. Smith
F. C. Snapes
G. Soanes
E. G. Somerville
E. Southgate, M.M.

E. L. Spindler
G. E. Spokes
T. S. Spokes
C. S. Stevens, M.M.
F. J. Stevens
R. J. Stratford
F. E. Steele
T. Street
S. Stroud
J. W. Stuart
A. L. Stuchbery
P. T. Sutton
W. Swift

J. Taft
J. Tagg
A. H. Taylor
F. J. Taylor
A. J. Thatcher
H. Thatcher
W. Thatcher
J. W. Thomson
C. H. Trillow
A. J. Trout

T. Tuckwell
W. H. Truscott
A. H. Tugwell
P. Tugwell
C. W. Turner
E. H. Turner
W. H. Turner

A. C. Upson

S. G. Varnell[1]
G. N. Viner

G. H. Wadham
C. E. Wakeling
W. H. Ward
D. R. Warner
F. Warwick
F. P. Watkins
W. S. J. Watts
A. E. Webb
F. B. Webber
C. W. Weblin
A. Wells

V. C. Weston
F. E. Whale
A. G. Wheeler
A. F. L. Wheeler
A. E. White
J. A. White
A. E. J. White
G. W. White
M. A. White
R. White
J. F. J. Whitehead
G. C. Whitmill
H. W. Wilder
W. J. Wilkins
R. H. Willis
E. B. Winstone
L. C. Winstone
H. J. Wise
J. H. Wood
A. G. Woodley
C. G. Woodwards
G. N. Wooldridge

T. R. Young